Expanding
Comprehension
With Multigenre Text Sets

Maria Nichols

■SCHOLASTIC

New York • Toronto • London • Auckland • Sydney
Mexico City • New Delhi • Hong Kong • Buenos Aires

Dedication

For my parents, who encouraged inquisitive habits of mind.

Acquiring editor: Lois Bridges
Developmental editor: Gloria Pipkin
Production management: Amy Rowe
Cover design: Brian LaRossa
Interior design: LDL Designs
Copy editor: Eileen Judge

ISBN-13: 978-0-545-10567-5
ISBN-10: 0-545-10567-6
Copyright © 2009 by Maria Nichols
All rights reserved. Published by Scholastic Inc.
Printed in the U.S.A.
1 2 3 4 5 6 7 8 9 10   40   15 14 13 12 11 10 09

Contents

Acknowledgments

Beware of the man of one book.
—Thomas Aquinas

For me, the grand finale to the act of writing is the process of thinking through the acknowledgments. I save them for last, not because words fail me, but because I cherish the opportunity to step back from the work and reflect, and because I want the time and space to revel in it.

In keeping with the heart of this text, my reflections begin with the people I count on to stretch my understanding of this world because of their propensity to read widely and deeply, push against what they read, and think and talk with others to construct bigger understandings. These are the friends and colleagues I trust to offer a differing perspective on new arenas of exploration, new sources to consider, and whole-heartedly engage in the co-construction of understanding. A peek into my in-box would reveal strings of ongoing electronic conversations with each, or in some cases, all of them. Each one of them faces the world with eager open-mindedness—and challenges me continually to do the same.

Although my work in the San Diego Unified District has sent me beyond the walls of Webster Elementary, I continue to think and learn alongside teachers Jeralyn Treas and Susie Althof. I look forward to the days I'm able to learn alongside them in their classrooms, knowing I'll leave with a multitude of thoughts to explore.

My new role in the San Diego Unified School District has vastly expanded my circle of colleagues. Thankfully, it has brought the opportunity for close collaboration with Doug McIntosh, an Ed-Tech imagineer who has me rethinking the role of technology in the twenty-first-century classroom. Together we're exploring the groundswell of possibilities that occur when technical know-how and strong instructional practices intersect.

I'm continually thankful to Debra Crouch for her friendship and her knack for propelling me endlessly toward new awareness. From the world of farmers markets to the reconsideration of accepted patterns of professional development, I know every e-mail and conversation with her offers the possibility of seeing the world differently. The same is true of Tiffiny Jackson, who offers camaraderie in exploring new avenues and angles on curricular design and professional development.

Peter Johnston has been kind enough to lend a critical eye to my ideas, pushing back at my thinking and continuously expanding my perspective. Gloria Pipkin and Lois Bridges have once again risen far above their primary roles as editors to offer guidance, encouragement, and invaluable feedback. I have everything a writer needs not only to sustain effort, but also to grow through the effort.

Additionally, I'm blessed to have family and close friends who encourage me toward my goals despite my all too frequent absences. Especially Rick, who supports me and even pretends to like Cheerios for dinner—thank you.

Foreword

The need for students to comprehend nonfiction has become a major focus in schools across the country. Educators recognize that if our students are to be successful, they need to be competent in critically navigating a rapidly changing world—a world that uses informational texts as its core language. What Maria Nichols does in this book is make us aware that these informational texts are not simply an array of facts that need to be learned and remembered. They are the collection of numerous perspectives that readers need to connect with, question, synthesize, and evaluate—thus forming their own understanding. As so perfectly stated by Maria,

> And, as we read widely and deeply, considering each source critically and navigating among them, comparing, contrasting, questioning, rereading and rethinking each, and drawing others in to think and talk with us, we are propelled toward the construction of new understandings.

Maria's approach to text sets challenges the notion that we can gain all our information from one source. For too long, especially in our science and social studies, we have used one text as the sole resource. As Maria so beautifully demonstrates, it is only through exposure to multiple sources of information—not just books, but magazines, newspapers, brochures, and media literacy—that we create a picture of our world. How wonderful it was to see that Maria has identified these sources as not just books, but also magazines, newspapers, brochures, and electronic media.

As I read through this text, I was heartened to see how Maria impresses upon her readers the importance of questioning and conversing to elevate students' comprehension. Her wonderful transcripts of classroom dialogue demonstrate the significant role of oral language in bringing students to greater meanings. Her emphasis on inquiry-based learning highlights the importance of students being in control of their own learning.

This is a book that every teacher needs to read. For too long nonfiction has been taught as the mindless reading and regurgitation of information presented within a set text. It has been a passive endeavor. As educators, if we are to truly help our students become analytical and critical readers who can understand multiple perspectives, then we need to make reading an active and interactive process that calls upon multiple sources. I commend Maria for writing this much needed and highly valuable resource. After reading this book, I was immediately motivated to critically look at my own classroom practices to ensure that I was not only giving students a wealth of varied sources to tap into, but also encouraging them to interact with and compare the sources to gain a more critical perspective.

—Tony Stead
April 2009

Chapter 1

Learning to Live Thoughtfully in the World

Why We Need to Read, Think, and Talk Among Multiple Sources of Information

> Few people are capable of expressing with equanimity opinions
> which differ from the prejudices of their social environments.
> Most people are even incapable of forming such opinions.
> ~ Albert Einstein

KENNY: Mrs. Nichols, why did they do it?

As I turned my head slowly to face Kenny, I searched my mind for possibilities. Yesterday's playground incident? The company who delivered the wrong bookshelves to the classroom? But it was the morning of Sept. 12, 2001, and in my heart I knew that neither playground squabbles nor errant bookshelves were what Kenny was struggling to comprehend. Before I was able to stumble through what was sure to be an inadequate response, Marco weighed in.

MARCO: My dad watched the news, and they said it's because some people—they don't like us.

ISSY: Yeah, we watched it, too. And, my mom and me looked in the newspaper, and it showed how the planes went—on purpose.

MANNY: Did you read any other kinda stuff? So you know if it's true?

KENNY: Yeah—so we can know why?

Using Multiple Sources to Construct an Understanding of a Complex World

It seems that the complexity of today's world demands that we navigate intricate global issues with no clear-cut "right" course of action. From immigration to energy, foreign policy to religious conflict, economic and cultural forces to social revolution, we as a global community are juggling differing perspectives and values that at times seem to know no common ground.

And as issues go, these children, second graders whose biggest worries should have been playground squabbles and missing bookshelves, were struggling to understand something most adults are still grappling with today. At that moment, the children had no answers, nor did I. Yet, as I think back to Manny's question, I'm realizing that what these children did have was a beginning awareness of the process we must engage in to understand, a habit of mind we had been developing over the course of our previous year together by consistently reading, thinking, and talking among multiple sources of information.

Did you read any other kinda stuff? So you know if it's true? How many of us, adults that we are, watched and listened in those first minutes, first hours, first days and weeks after 9/11, waiting for others to tell us why? Did *I* pause to wonder what other sources *I* might consult, so *I know if it's true, so I can know why?*

With the interconnectedness brought about by globalization comes an increased awareness of global issues and a realization that these issues touch us all. Listen, and seemingly everyone has an opinion about the array of challenges we face. But listen closely, and what becomes clear is that these opinions are too frequently formed from quick bits of information gleaned from single sources, whether they are sound bites from the evening news, the ranting of self-proclaimed talk-show experts, the headlines of a single newspaper, or a chat with like-minded friends. And even where multiple sources have been consulted, they are most often sources closely in keeping with the belief system of the individual, consulted with the intent of confirmation as opposed to questioning and strengthening understanding.

Rarely do we encounter an individual who has an in-depth and balanced grasp of any one issue, someone who understands the issue from multiple perspectives, knows how and why it evolved, and has suggestions for clear, feasible actions that may have a positive impact on the course of events. Such an understanding is rare because of the process required to achieve it.

Affecting a positive course of action with the global issues we face requires energy, effort, time, and open-minded inquiry across a multitude of sources of information, *so we can know why* and *how*. Many adults, let alone children, simply do not have the inclination, open-mindedness, stamina, or ability to search out and critically comprehend the array of sources of information required to gain a wide lens on issues, think among the sources, and talk purposefully with others to drive their understanding deeper.

Yet the use of multiple sources is crucial in that so much of what is posed as balanced information today is shaped by authors with purposes other than simply informing. In fact, just consulting multiple sources without checking the voice, the driving force behind each source, is no longer enough. In 1996 Congress passed the Telecommunications Act, which lifted some restrictions on previous laws designed to protect markets from sole access to a single voice. Relaxation of the "One-to-a-Market Rule" allows corporations to own multiple radio and television stations in a single market. This removal of restrictions on media ownership creates increased potential for corporate domination of the airwaves. As the lyrics to John Mayer's "Waiting on the World to Change" warn us,

And when you trust your television
What you get is what you got
Cause when they own the information, oh
They can bend it all they want.

Becoming Purposefully Literate

Paulo Freire, Brazilian educator and proponent of critical pedagogy, describes literacy as an active phenomenon. He argues, "Its power lies not in a perceived ability to read and write, but rather in an individual's capacity to put these skills to work in shaping the course of his or her life" (1970, p. 12). Being purposefully literate, as Freire suggests, supposes the realization that we continuously use our abilities to read, write, speak, and listen as a means of constructing and interpreting meaning in every aspect of our interactions with the world. And, in a flat and increasingly interconnected world, we must add the realization that we have the power to use our constructed understandings as social empowerment, as a force to be used to shape the course of lives far beyond our own.

Learning to read, think, and talk among sources of information in order to navigate and build an understanding of our world is an essential, foundational ability for becoming purposefully literate. We don't read to understand texts; we read to understand *ideas*. Rarely do we succeed in this quest by relying on single sources of information in isolation.

Rather, this quest to understand and act on our understanding requires us to pursue ideas across multiple texts of varying genres and media forms. It sends us on a journey of thought which allows us to explore issues and ideas in depth. And, as we read widely and deeply, considering each source critically and navigating among them, comparing, contrasting, questioning, rereading and rethinking each, and drawing others in to think and talk with us, we are propelled toward the construction of new understandings. It is the application of understandings from single sources to other sources and situations, and the synthesis of newly constructed understandings that allow us to craft our own beliefs about the world. This is the process that brings new insights, and with these insights, innovation. Only when we understand with this depth are we able to act upon and shape our world thoughtfully; only then are we truly becoming purposefully literate.

My good friend and passionate social crusader Debra Crouch uses her tenacity as a reader not only to observe the world, but also to motivate participation with an attitude toward change. Debra has pulled me into yet another book, and consequently another interwoven network of ideas, in the same way she always does—by reading aloud or e-mailing thought-provoking excerpts of whatever she is elbow deep in. Debra's hook this time was a quote from *The End of Poverty: Economic Possibilities for Our Time* (2005). The author, Jeffrey Sachs, suggests, "The beauty of ideas is that they can be used over and over again, without ever being depleted" (p. 41).

Who could resist that? As I waded into this text, and by default, into the issue of poverty, I quickly realized this is an issue no one, single source of information can possibly enable me to grasp, nor is it an issue around which I should limit my developing understanding to a single point of view. Now, sitting next to the first source of information are a stack of other titles, including *The Bottom Billion: Why the Poorest Countries Are Failing and What Can Be Done About It* by Paul Collier, and *Development as Freedom* by Amartya Sen. In addition, I've been scouring online sources such as Nobel Peace Prize winner Muhammad Yunus's Web site, which chronicles an effort to engage in the issue of poverty in a truly innovative way (http://muhammadyunus.org).

Essentially, Debra's original recommendation ignited not only a heightened awareness, but a boiling cauldron of unanswered questions, and a driving need to know. Thanks to Amazon.com's marketing genius (*Customers who bought this item also bought* . . .) and the power of Google, I'm in the midst of gathering multiple sources of information, preparing for a journey of thought propelled by reading and thinking and talking with a wide range of colleagues. To deepen my understanding, I've been actively seeking out conversations with those I find to be like-minded, as they support my efforts to articulate the thoughts swirling in my head. Conversely, I'm also reveling in conversations with those who tend to approach issues from a different stance than I, as they push at my thinking, forcing me to question assumptions and confront flaws in my logic.

As I construct understanding of the issue and the ideas of those also struggling with the issue, I'm developing a heightened sense of purpose. I am reading not only to know why, but to know how, as one cannot possibly work to comprehend this issue and engage with the ideas born from the struggle and not be compelled to act—to use literacy as Freire insists we must.

PREPARING FOR A CONTINUALLY EVOLVING ECONOMIC LANDSCAPE

The workplace our children will encounter when they leave our classrooms is evolving in directions about which we can only hypothesize. Consequently, our children are preparing for jobs that don't yet exist and, if recent history is predictive, may well become obsolete during their working lifetime.

Despite all the unknowns, what **is** known is that the skill set children will need to succeed will be based on the ability to access and synthesize large amounts of information; think collectively, critically, and flexibly; problem solve in novel situations; and communicate with clarity. As Clay Shirky, author and expert on the social and economic effects of Internet technologies, observes, "We are living in the middle of the largest increase in expressive capability in the history of the human race" (2008, p. 106). This information revolution has created a world where the importance of having information is overshadowed by the ability to think about and use information. To make sense of our world and function, we must construct operable understandings from the explosion of information we constantly receive.

In *Five Minds for the Future* (2006), Howard Gardner discusses the kinds of minds our children will need to thrive in the world of the future, pointing out that it "will demand capacities that until now have been mere options" (p. 2). Among these capacities, he includes the ability to think through and synthesize the overwhelming multitude of information now available and to use it in meaningful ways.

Gardner defines the synthesizing mind as one that "takes information from disparate sources, understands and evaluates that information objectively, and puts it together in ways that make sense to the synthesizer and also to other persons" (p. 3). He postulates that those who do not have the ability to synthesize information will be overwhelmed by information and unable to make decisions.

Not surprisingly, we see evidence of a need for these abilities in the workplace structures and practices of the most innovative companies today. In *The Art of Innovation* (2001), authors Tom Kelley and Jonathan Littman share the story of IDEO, one of the world's leading design firms and the brain trust behind an extensive list of brilliant innovations, including the Apple mouse, the insulin pen, and my personal favorite—the stand-up, no-squeeze toothpaste tube. At the heart of IDEO's innovative method is the project-specific, temporary formation of "hot teams," which are flexible groups of individuals from widely divergent disciplines. Founder David Kelley asserts, "Quite simply, great projects are achieved by great teams" (p. 69).

IDEO's hot teams are deliberately composed of individuals from widely varying backgrounds because the range in their arenas of expertise brings not only a range of knowledge, but differentiated lenses through which each challenge is viewed. Team participation requires abilities vastly different from the working world perpetuated by Dilbert cartoons, including the ability to think and talk purposefully among large quantities of information from disparate sources, distill and synthesize the important bits, and apply those ideas to unique situations.

IDEO is not alone is recognizing the power of teams. The Discovery channel's *Modern Marvels* is fast becoming my favorite source for examples of the power of collaborative efforts and conversations. While some of the ideas highlighted on the show, which features noteworthy innovations, enterprises and inventions, are the brainchild of single geniuses, far more are born from constructive conversations and collaborative efforts among people with varied backgrounds but a shared passion.

In both IDEO and the innovative efforts highlighted on *Modern Marvels*, we are offered a glimpse at the skills and strategies necessary to excel in the knowledge-based economy: the ability to sift through and synthesize large amounts of information; talk purposefully to navigate differing points of view and generate newer, bigger ideas; and work collaboratively to transform these ideas into a reality.

The challenges of changing work environments and the abilities required to participate successfully are echoed by the authors of *Tough Choices or Tough Times: The Report of the New Commission on the Skills of the American Workforce* (2006). They describe a world in which "comfort with ideas and abstractions is the passport to a good job, in which creativity and innovation are the key to the good life, in which high levels of education—a very different kind of education than most of us have had—are going to be the only security there is" (p. xviii).

While we can't choose our children's economic future, certainly we must be sure to design learning experiences that prepare them with the attitudes and abilities necessary to take a seat at the table if they so choose.

PREPARING FOR A PARTICIPATORY DEMOCRACY

A successful democracy necessitates the collective actions of a thoughtful, purposeful group of people working to achieve a common goal; a way of life that allows for specific qualities and freedoms. Democracy cannot prevail when people entrusted with its evolution don't make intelligent, altruistic decisions. Every level of involvement in a democracy, from voting to serving as an elected official, requires an in-depth understanding of issues and their effect on our way of life, the ability to consider many possible courses of action, and the capacity to contemplate the probable results of each.

The beginnings of the 2008 presidential race highlighted the need for thoughtful, critically persistent public engagement. A stunning array of candidates with unprecedented diversity vied for America's attention and support—both action-based and financial.

The campaigns themselves required extraordinary amounts of money, much of which was spent on market research and media blitzes, with testing of sound bites to gauge public reaction prior to the mass media efforts. New forms of media, such as YouTube, were used to engage and impress a wider segment of the public. Candidates staged press opportunities to carefully craft their image, rehearsed for all

Expanding Comprehension With Multigenre Text Sets

possible scenarios in debates, and even planned their wardrobe based on the audience for public events, from formal speeches to factory tours.

So, how do we get to know the individual behind the carefully crafted image? Or, do we? How many Americans vote based on shallow impressions gleaned from television ads or biased news programming? How many even realize that these news sources have a bias, based on their own financial backing? How many read candidates' position statements, trace their voting records to determine whether their actions support their claims, and compare statements and information released in differing media outlets for differing audiences for consistency? And how many read and listen to diverse opinions, talk purposefully with people from differing perspectives, and think among all these sources to synthesize a sense of the person and form their own educated opinion? Just imagine the outcome of a presidential election in which voters prepared and participated in this way simply because understanding the candidates, platforms, and issues demanded it!

Let's move beyond elections to the foundation of our democracy—the premise of a government by the people and for the people. The World Wide Web has become a spark rekindling grassroots organizations of old—groups of individuals who share a common passion and work from the bottom up to effect change.

Wecansolveit.org is one of the latest examples of digital grassroots activism, created to unite people from varying backgrounds and arenas of expertise in an effort to ignite a national conversation on the issue of climate change. However, it's joined by a range of Web sites focused on alternative energy, some of which are authored by entities vying for entry into the alternate-energy technology arena for less than altruistic reasons. It's up to the reader to determine the voice behind the message, to discern who's in this for the good of our planet, and who's in it for a quick profit or control of what may possibly be the oil-boom equivalent of the twenty-first century.

From Web sites to flash mobs, the digital networking age has ushered in opportunities to participate in the democratic process in ways our founding fathers couldn't possibly have imagined. Adding one's voice to these and other conversations in thoughtful ways requires not only wading through large amounts of information and opinions on Web sites, but also expanding these understandings by searching out and thinking among a range of other sources of information. Knowing this, we must be certain we are preparing our children to construct the understanding required to participate in these grassroots conversations, digital or otherwise, so they are able to take part in shaping policy decisions in ways that strengthen both our society and our democratic spirit.

Defining Literacy (and Literacy Instruction) in the Twenty-first Century

In a speech delivered at Harvard University in 1943, Winston Churchill proclaimed, "the empires of the future are the empires of the mind." More than 65 years later, this truth still holds strong. Certainly, understanding complex issues and ideas in the twenty-first century requires the ability to think. It requires that individuals are able to access and think among large amounts of information in many media forms, respond critically, synthesize, talk purposefully with others, and construct meaning. This realization has a profound impact on the way we define what it means to understand, and the way we teach comprehension.

Yet this sometimes messy process of thinking and constructing understanding is not what we find in classrooms. A peek inside classrooms across America reveals children being taught to rely on single, traditional texts as a means of contemplating issues and ideas. Comprehension is defined along a continuum of understanding, ranging from literal recall to rich, critical evaluations of big ideas—but inside these single texts. Comprehension instruction is designed as a progression of strategies practiced inside these single texts whose ideas are considered in isolation from other texts. Even when strategies are taught as a medley of interwoven cognitive processes aimed at critical understandings of big ideas, their use remains bound within a single text, rather than as a means of expanding understanding by pursuing ideas through many sources of information.

Not surprisingly, then, research reveals that many high school students lack the ability to think among multiple sources of information and then to synthesize in order to construct new understandings (Ogle & Blachowitz, 2002; Afflerbach & VanSledright, 1998; Wineburg 1991). A study by Simpson and Nist (2002) revealed that, when presented with multiple sources, students tended to read and think through each text as a separate entity, often not even noticing contradictions. Simpson and Nist attributed this to an accumulation of learning experiences in the elementary years involving single texts in a transmission model of instruction. Moje (1996) and Jetton (1994) add that children who learn in such environments learn passivity; they simply don't understand their role in the construction of meaning.

This passivity as learners, combined with the simple fact that children have not been taught how to purposefully read, think, and talk among multiple sources of information, offers some insight into the struggles our high school students display (Shanahan, 2003). Blachowitz and Ogle (2001) emphasize that a process for constructing understanding among multiple sources must become part of our comprehension instruction. To enable success, they suggest, we must help children form a habit of reading and thinking among several sources to verify and clarify information. But verifying and clarifying information is not enough. To be literate in the twenty-first century, children must use this information to construct their own understandings of issues and ideas, and develop the propensity to act on these understandings.

In *To Understand*, Ellin Keene identifies the exploration of ideas across multiple sources of information as a pivotal dimension in developing understanding for learners of all ages (2008). The journey of thought we undertake as we read, think, and talk among multiple sources of information is not separate from the comprehension of single sources of information; rather, it enables a deepening of comprehension as single sources are revisited through a lens widened by other sources. This aligns with a constructivist theory of learning, which supports pedagogy that encourages children toward active construction of knowledge as opposed to the passive absorption of information dispensed by expert others. The active construction of knowledge is a process that must be practiced to the degree that learning in this way becomes a habit of mind.

Designing curriculum for reading, thinking, and talking among sources of information, then, requires us to explore the content of our literacy instruction from kindergarten on. It requires that we expand our goals for strong comprehension, broaden our definition of text, and rethink the process required to truly understand.

When we broaden our comprehension instruction, amplifying children's ability to understand by teaching them to use multiple sources to expand comprehension of single sources, and then use the resulting constructed meaning purposefully to develop their understanding of larger ideas or issues in the world, we are able to develop the skill set children will need to succeed in the developing workplace and in furthering our democratic way of life.

When drawing from multiple sources of information, we must support children in rethinking their purpose for reading, viewing it as an opportunity to construct or reconstruct beliefs as opposed to gathering discrete facts (which, depending on the source, may or may not be grounded in truth). It requires that we teach children how to read critically for deep meaning in all genres and media forms; that we consider how reading, thinking, and talking among a variety of genres and media forms supports readers in constructing stronger understandings; and that we teach children the power of purposeful talk. It also requires a slowing down to truly think about and synthesize information and ideas. This slowing down is crucial, for, as Ellin Keene asks, "Do we demonstrate our lofty goals by asking children to fly through hundreds of books, with little expectation that they dwell in ideas or learn more?" (2008, p. 14).

Through the pages of this book, we'll investigate instruction that supports and encourages children to approach complex issues and ideas by engaging in a process that helps them to *know if it's true* and persist *so they can know why*. We'll explore supporting children in learning to read, think, and talk among multiple sources of information for the purpose of constructing stronger understanding of issues and ideas. We will delve into the role of talk, the use of text sets, and the creation of units of study that incorporate instruction along the release of responsibility continuum to build independent ability.

In discussing this work, we'll listen in on the conversations of children from a variety of teachers at Webster Elementary, an urban public school in a lower socioeconomic neighborhood in the San Diego Unified School District. I had the privilege of serving as literacy coach for four years at Webster, studying purposeful talk, lesson design, and instructional practices alongside an incredible range of passionate professionals. To illustrate the work described in the chapters to come, we'll closely follow the instructional flow and lesson design in Jeralyn Treas's third-grade classroom and visit my own classroom prior to my foray into coaching.

Former South African President Nelson Mandela once said, "Education is the most powerful weapon you can use to change the world." While many of the political, environmental, religious, social, economic, and cultural issues facing us today may not be appropriate topics for our children, surely the habits of mind necessary to think and reason through complex issues with no clear right answer or one agreed-upon course of action, and the propensity to use constructed understandings to act on and live in our world in more thoughtful ways, must become the overarching goal of our reading comprehension instruction. Perhaps our mission was best captured by Franklin D. Roosevelt in a 1941 speech at the University of Pennsylvania: "We cannot always build the future for our youth, but we can build the youth for our future."

Chapter 2

Creating a Literacy of Thoughtfulness

> To be able to be caught up into the world of
> thought—that is being educated.
> ~Edith Hamilton

I was leaving the gym early one Saturday, and tuned in to National Public Radio, hoping to laugh along with *Car Talk* as I drove. Instead, I caught the tail end of *Weekend Edition*. Host Scott Simon was interviewing Judge Richard Posner, of the U.S. Court of Appeals, Seventh Circuit, Chicago, and author of *Uncertain Shield: The U.S. Intelligence System in the Throes of Reform*. The conversation was focused on terrorism, and the question posed was whether the restructuring of the U.S. Intelligence community was truly an improvement, or simply a political reaction. It was not the topic that caught my attention, but the way Judge Posner had been introduced. Simon welcomed Posner as a prolific writer and thinker. A prolific writer? Impressive, yet I had heard that honor bestowed upon others. But a prolific thinker? A more honorable homage, I could not imagine. Who was this prolific thinker, I wondered? What words of wisdom would a prolific thinker impart? How does one become a prolific thinker? What course of experiences creates the necessary habits of mind? And most important, do we dare hold out this possibility for ourselves and our children?

Curiosity being what it is, I Googled Judge Posner, and quickly came across his Web site. My eyes spinning from the compilation of degrees and honors, I took refuge in a listing of his publications down the side of the page. My first reaction was simply to count—38. Whew—prolific writer indeed! Then, I began to note the topics. As you might expect, there were numerous titles on law, the focus of which ranged from plagiarism to intellectual property rights, legal theory to antitrust law, and on to elections, constitutional law, bankruptcy, presidential impeachments, sex laws, and monopolies. But as if there weren't enough breadth and range of expertise in the legal titles, the list expanded to several titles on domestic intelligence, plus two titles on aging. And that's not all. As Graham Allison of the *Washington Post* quipped (2005), "Finding the puzzles presented by his day job on the U.S. Court of Appeals for the Seventh Circuit insufficiently challenging . . . ," Posner had penned a title on mega-disasters.

As I scrolled through Amazon.com to peruse Posner's work, a definition of a prolific thinker began to take shape: an impression of an individual who is actively and endlessly curious about his world, who allows this curiosity to propel him into intellectual pursuits far beyond his arena of expertise. I imagined a passionate and critical questioner of situations and information, confident in the face of intellectual challenges. I wondered about Judge Posner's method of immersion, the range of sources he draws from, and the circle of individuals he talks with to sharpen and expand his thinking. I was curious whether his training as a judge created the inclination to critically entertain divergent points of view from the multiple sources he encountered in the construction of his own opinion.

Conditions That Support Thoughtful Learning

"Learning is a consequence of thinking" (Perkins, 1992, p. 8). Leave it to David Perkins to offer such a simple yet profound foundational truth. Posner may well be a living expression of this assertion. Whether or not one agrees with the positions Judge Posner takes in his numerous publications, it would be difficult to argue with Simon's labeling of him as a prolific thinker, and his publications are certainly a testament to his range and prowess as a learner.

Perkins expands on his simple truth, pointing out that "this single sentence turns topsy-turvy the conventional pattern of schooling." He calls for thoughtful learning, which focuses "not just on schooling memories but on schooling minds" (p. 7). In its 2008 report, *Tough Choices or Tough Times*, the National Center on Education and the Economy echoes the assertion that schools need to be turned, in Perkin's words, topsy-turvy. The report emphasizes the urgent need for all Americans to be not only better educated but also differently educated. The N.C.E.E. challenges schools to shift from teaching and testing lower-order memory and analytic skills to teaching children to deal easily with abstractions and ideas. In essence, the report emphasizes the necessity of teaching children to think.

If we believe in the tenacity of the linkage between thinking and learning, then our goal must be to create what Rexford Brown describes as a literacy of thoughtfulness (1991), one in which children are caught up in a world of thought. This challenge leads us to an obvious question: How do we design learning environments and instructional opportunities that create a literacy of thoughtfulness?

Thoughtful learning occurs when children are asked to not only think about what they are learning but also to think with what they are learning. Perkins points to thoughtful learning as the means towards achieving the goal of generative knowledge, that is, knowledge that actually serves the learner in his or her pursuit of larger goals.

When we create learning experiences in which children pursue ideas by immersing themselves in reading, thinking, and talking critically among multiple sources of information, we are asking them to use what they learn to construct larger understandings about their world. We are creating the conditions and opportunities that require them to develop as thinkers. Surely individuals who thrive daily in instructional environments that encourage them to approach topics, issues, and ideas with an expectation of diverse sources of information with varied points of view and purposes behind them are immersed in thought. Individuals who actively search out these sources, read through a critical lens, think and talk with others, seek to understand their arena of curiosity from every angle, and synthesize what they have learned, are constructing the habits of mind that create both prolific thinkers and innovative spirits.

Foundational to a literacy of thoughtfulness are ways of thriving in a learning environment, behaviors and attitudes that are necessary to initiate and sustain learning and strengthen thinking. Notably, the constructive use of purposeful talk, the nurturing of curiosity and questions, the development of critical thinking, and a willingness to embrace a challenge must be emphasized. Teaching these behaviors and attitudes as deliberately as we teach content is necessary for our children's success in the world.

BUILDING PURPOSEFUL TALK

During the course of our day, we engage in a variety of types of talk for a variety of purposes. We can't always compartmentalize our interactions as being solely comprised of one type of talk; often we weave in and out of varying forms, depending on the course of the interaction and our goal for engaging in the interaction in the first place.

Just this morning, my husband, Rick, looked up from the Sunday paper, coffee in hand, a sly smile on his face, with the suggestion that we plan a holiday get-away to Palm Springs. He'd obviously been thinking about this for a while, as he had his argument well rehearsed: I needed—no, deserved—time off; we'd had little time together in the last few months; and, with the economy in its current state, rates just might be reasonable. His persuasive one-sided talk soon gave way to a more conversational give and take as we talked through what we might do if we gave in to the splurge: play golf, hike in Joshua Tree National Park, eat at our favorite restaurants, and then hike some more to make up for the favorite restaurants. The thoughts about hiking led to loosely related story talk from Rick about his recent rock climbing trip. As I listened, nagging guilt around commitments crept into my head, and I interrupted with interrogatory talk: How many days could we realistically plan for? What about other obligations? Before New Year's, or after? What about . . . ? How would we . . . ?

As with our family and social lives, classroom life is predicated upon a variety of types of talk. As Courtney Cazden reminds us, "the basic purpose of school is achieved through communication." Cazden asserts that the quality of learning depends on the quality of the communication system, a factor in which type of talk is used (2001, p. 2).

In *Life in a Crowded Place* (1992), Ralph Peterson highlights some of the types of talk we're apt to find in classrooms. In an emotionally healthy classroom, we're sure to find caring talk—the type of talk we use to greet each other and show concern. Story talk certainly plays a role as we share our life experiences. And, casual conversation—talking for the sheer delight of it and of each other—obviously builds strong bonds.

Yet, Peterson points out that, even with casual conversation, "There is no 'thing' to be given specific attention; there is no purpose beyond the lively participation and enjoyment of those involved" (p. 50). He points to another form of talk, which he labels "discussion," as the type of talk that allows learners to draw together in the pursuit of understanding. "In discussion, students always focus their attention on some 'thing' in order to know and understand" (p. 49).

Peterson's discussion is a constructive type of talk, much like what David Bohm labels "dialogue." In *On Dialogue* (2004), Bohm describes this type as talk in which people think together, taking part in creating a common meaning (p. 27). In her work with the Institute for Learning, Lauren Resnick (1999) refers to this focused, constructive talk as "accountable talk," noting that participants need to be accountable to the knowledge being constructed, to standards of reasoning, and to the learning community.

Courtney Cazden observes that this constructive talk often begins with exploratory talk—children "speaking without the answer fully intact" (p. 170). However, she notes that this exploratory talk then gives way to more fluent exchanges as the children use those tentative thoughts as a basis for constructing meaning together.

When children are taught to use talk purposefully to grow ideas and negotiate meaning, they develop habits for engaged, active construction of meaning. These interactions create not only purposeful interdependence, but also patterns for strong independent thinking.

It is this talk—discussion, dialogue, accountable talk, exploratory talk giving way to the fluid escalation of co-constructed ideas—that I refer to as purposeful talk (Nichols, 2006, 2008). And it is this talk that must permeate every interaction as children learn to read, think, and talk among multiple sources of information. Learning environments alive with purposeful talk nurture prolific thinkers.

ENCOURAGING CURIOSITY AND QUESTIONS

Curiosity and the resulting questions spring from a propensity to live in the world with wide-awake eyes. Through curiosity and questions, children develop interests and passions, which fuel thinking and the desire to learn. At times we are lucky enough to glimpse curiosity in action.

Let's listen in on a brief conversation with Maritza and Stephanie. This particular morning, the two sixth graders rushed into their classroom ahead of their classmates, and made a beeline for the classroom library. The teacher and I spied them busily scrambling through texts, their backpacks and jackets discarded in the general vicinity of their desks. It was too much to resist—I had to find out what they were up to.

MARIA: What are you two so excited over?

MARITZA: Well see, Stephanie saw this movie on TV, and she said it was like this book (holding up a copy of *The Wall* by Eve Bunting). They're both about people not getting along and having a war. And we were talking about it, and then, we remembered this other book—this one—

(holding up a copy of *Christmas in the Trenches* by John McCutcheon) was also about people not getting along, because they had a war. And there's all these, too (pointing to a haphazard pile of quickly pulled books on the floor at her feet, which included *So Far From the Sea* by Eve Bunting and *The Bracelet* by Yoshiko Uchida).

STEPHANIE: And the news talks all about the war now. It got us curious because we want to know why it gets so bad that we have wars.

MARIA: How do you think the books will help?

STEPHANIE: Well, it's like—the books— we can use them to see how the characters feel.

MARITZA: And to see how bad the world was so they had to have a war. We don't get how everything's so bad. Why can't they just talk and get better?

Is there room at the U.N. for two sixth graders? What's so compelling here is that a movie (the title of which I was never able to pin down) sparked a thought, an unsettled sense of the world, in Stephanie. She did what anyone curious and wrestling with dissonance does—she shared her thoughts with a friend. The two translated their curiosity into an action propelled by a question, and were compiling resources to support the formation of theories. This inquiry will involve the two in an intense study of a range of sources of information at very deep levels, questioning authors' messages and the ways of the world. They will use what they learn to pursue ideas and to shape their understanding of their world and their actions. I had no doubt that the end result, whether Stephanie and Maritza found an explanation that satisfied them or not, would be far more advanced than that of children who were assigned a similar exploration.

Now, wouldn't it be grand if all of our students burst through our door each morning brimming with their own self-generated questions and propelled themselves into worlds of thought as we simply looked on with awe? But we know that, to support and offer visions of possibility, we must offer learning experiences carefully designed to provoke curiosity. From this curiosity, questions will flow—questions that propel the learner into a world of inquiry, as evidenced by Stephanie and Maritza.

Of course, creating this requires thoughtful planning and an understanding of what sparks curiosity and the resulting questions. I visited a fifth-grade reading workshop in the second day of a study, and was surprised to find an odd mix of energized engagement and idle detachment in the children. One pair of students in particular was sitting listlessly, staring at a pile of reptile books. These were gorgeous books, filled with stunning photos, enticing page layouts, and eye-catching charts and graphs. But the girls were not touching the books. Needless to say, this partnership was my first stop.

MARIA: What are you two doing?

TANYA: Trying to make up a question.

MARIA: Why are you making up a question?

SHERALYN: We can't read until we have a question.

MARIA: What are you wondering?

SHERALYN: We don't know because we don't know a lot about reptiles. I think we can ask if a snake is a reptile, but Tanya already says it is one.

Children sitting in lethargic silence, stuck because they can't make up a question? I thought of myself just that morning, late running out of the house because I took fifteen minutes to scan the newspaper. Those few precious minutes allowed me to semi-immerse myself in a range of issues, including recounts and opinions on fighting in Xuahaca, the plight of orphaned black bear cubs in Alaska, elephants stampeding in Indonesia, diminishing populations of fish in our oceans, and proposed restrictions on renting to undocumented immigrants. I read just enough to fill my head with questions as I drove to work. If all the fish are disappearing, what's the future of ocean mammals that depend on them for food? Are all fish disappearing, or just certain species? What motivates some people to restrict access to others? What's distressing the elephants? Since elephants are intelligent and social, are the stampedes organized and purposeful? Are diseases affecting the bear populations? Is it hunting season? What diseases kill black bears? What caused the strife in Xuahaca? Social issues, economic, political, a mix of all three? Admittedly, some of my questions were rather narrow, but still, I couldn't imagine having to make up questions. These questions came without effort. So what was the difference?

The most obvious possibility is that my questions weren't forced, and I didn't have to make them up prior to exposure. Rather, exposure—minimal as it was—ignited curiosity, and the questions flowed. Sure enough, investigation into this reading workshop revealed a similar situation. The children who had chosen a topic or issue because curiosity or passion had already developed elsewhere were off and running. Those who had ventured into an unknown topic, which was the case with the partnership I encountered that day, simply needed time to immerse and explore before questions could be expected to flow.

As we teach children to read, think, and talk among sources of information—as in all their learning endeavors—we want their efforts to be propelled by honest and challenging questions. All too often, however, we see children assigned the task of asking questions before they know enough to generate them. Forced questioning too early in the process, as we saw with Sheralyn and Tanya, often results in rote, surface-level questions, questions with simple answers that, once stated, halt momentum. However, when children are given time to explore topics and issues, they discover unique aspects or angles that appeal to them. Freedom to engage with an area of curiosity in their own way, focusing on these unique avenues, offers children a sense of control over and excitement about their learning. The result makes the notion of having to assign questions seem ridiculous.

For a case in point, let's peek into Stacie Wright's fifth-grade classroom. The children were elbow deep in a nonfiction study designed to support them in strengthening their ability to read, think, and talk among multiple sources of information. Within this study, the children were pursuing issues and ideas surrounding the American Revolution. The children started the process with time to explore a range of sources of information, letting curiosity build. At this point in their inquiry, the children were reading, thinking, and talking among sources in an initial text set to construct some base knowledge, and noting avenues of the Revolution which piqued their own curiosity.

I found Jessi curled in a corner of the room, surrounded by texts devoted to the colonies' black regiments. Jessi shared that she gathered these texts because she was startled to learn that slaves were allowed to fight. As she flipped through her initial sources, she wondered if their masters had forced them to fight, and if they had been allowed to use guns.

But as Jessi read and thought and talked with others, the depth of knowledge she was constructing allowed her questioning to take a more critical turn. Now she was wondering whether the soldiers were actually fighting for the colonies' freedom, or were more hopeful of winning their own freedom. With some knowledge under her belt, Jessi had formed a rich, multifaceted question which would require a range of sources of information. Answering her question would require a critical examination of these sources, much thinking and talking with others, and a synthesis of information, leading her eventually to develop ideas far richer than anything conveyed in any one of these sources alone. Jessi would be thinking not only about the information she was learning but also with the information she was learning to construct new understandings.

This is the way we want our children to generate and use questions—not as a compliance task, but as the result of exposure to sources of information and instructional experiences that serve as a catalyst for curiosity, igniting a need to read, think, and talk among multiple sources of information.

DEVELOPING THE ABILITY TO THINK CRITICALLY

In the age of blogs, Web sites, and numerous other venues for publishing just about anything an individual might care to, literal-level understanding or unquestioned acceptance of deeper ideas in texts can no longer pass for comprehension. Children must learn to listen and read with a critical stance, questioning each source they encounter, questioning the author's intent as well as his or her qualifications to speak on the topic, issue, or ideas under consideration. As P. David Pearson suggests, "comprehension is never enough; it must have a critical edge" (2001).

In *Asking the Right Questions: A Guide to Critical Thinking* (2004), authors Browne and Keeley look beyond the questions born from curiosity to focused, critical questions that help us to engage thoughtfully with the information we discover and enable us to make decisions about its validity and worth. Browne and Keeley regard reading or listening without questioning as essentially absorbing another's opinion as one's own. It results in what they refer to as opinions, beliefs, and decisions that are "accidents of association" (p. 4). This lack of thinking for oneself is not only paralyzing for an individual, but for society as well. This stance is echoed by Jerome Harste, who argues that children must become "agents of text rather than victims of text" (2006, p. 18).

Alan Luke and Peter Freebody framed comprehension as consisting of four roles, shown in Figure 2.1, which readers must master to lead literate lives in the twenty-first century (1990). As readers engage with texts across all four roles, they are nudged out of literal understandings and propelled toward the critical understandings necessary for deep comprehension.

Figure 2.1: THE FOUR ROLES OF READERS

Role	Reader Action
Code Breaker	How do I crack the code of this text? Readers use their understanding of the code of written language, including alphabetic knowledge, spelling, sounds in words, and structural conventions and patterns, to decode and encode language.
Text Participant	What does this text mean? Readers understand that texts convey meaning and use their knowledge of the world and the ways language works to comprehend and compose texts.
Text User	What do I do with this text here and now? Readers understand and craft texts using their understanding of specific social contexts.
Text Analyst	What is this text trying to do to me? The reader recognizes that texts are not neutral, and critically analyzes texts to determine author's point of view and range of influence.

Drawing on his research on reading primary source documents inside the history domain, Sam Wineburg emphasizes the importance of working towards understanding what a text is attempting to do (2001, p. 65). As with Luke and Freebody's assertions about the role of text analyst, Wineburg argues that only when we know what a text is attempting to do are we in a position to judge the information inside.

To support children in becoming text analysts, as Luke and Freebody and Wineburg advocate, Browne and Keeley suggest the use of a systematic evaluation of sources of information, explaining that, "Critical thinking consists of an awareness of a set of interrelated critical questions, plus the ability and willingness to ask and answer them at appropriate times" (p. 3). The questions they suggest are listed in Figure 2.2.

When teachers raise these questions on a daily basis, model their thinking, encourage children to think

Figure 2.2: CRITICAL QUESTIONS

1. What are the issues and conclusions?
2. What are the reasons?
3. Which words or phrases are ambiguous?
4. What are the value conflicts and assumptions?
5. Are there any fallacies in the reasoning?
6. How good is the evidence?
7. Are there rival causes?
8. Are the statistics deceptive?
9. What significant information is omitted?
10. What reasonable conclusions are possible?

From *Asking the Right Questions* by M. Neil Browne and Stuart B. Keeley, page 13.

alongside them, and use thinking from other sources to push against the author's ideas, they will help children learn the role of text analysts. When children are reminded to ask these questions as they read, and to think and talk in these ways on their own, the habits of mind for thinking critically will form.

This is the level of awareness, and of thinking and talking, we are building toward from kindergarten on. Even our youngest learners live in a world where they are continuously bombarded with texts attempting to act upon them for a purpose. As Luke notes, "the coming of the Internet has exposed students who are just old enough to click a mouse to whatever arguments anyone with access to a computer wishes to aim at them" (1994).

As we teach children to pursue ideas by reading, thinking, and talking among multiple sources of information, we must design lessons that not only build stronger critical thinking inside each text but that also do it across sources, noting the range of perspectives represented. Children who make every effort to include multiple perspectives will have a wider context to support efforts at critical analysis of each source, and will be better able to shape a well-informed opinion of their own.

Of course, it's not always possible to gather texts for children that represent a range of perspectives. Consider, for example, Ben Franklin. I was sitting with a group of third graders who were reading, thinking, and talking about Ben.

MANUEL: Mrs. Nichols, all these authors say the same thing about Benjamin Franklin— that he was good and smart and heroic. We don't have another point of view to think about.

As I scanned the array of texts the trio had strewn about them, I knew that Manuel was right. While adult texts ventured into some of Ben's digressions, texts intended for children were certainly not going to offer a hint of their possibility.

MARIA: Do you think it's possible that he was truly all good?

ALL: No!

ALANI: No one's perfect. Everybody—even us—makes mistakes.

MARIA: So why don't any of these authors discuss this? Why do they all have this same point of view about Ben?

All three look at each other.

Manuel: Well—it may be like because what he did that made him famous is so good—

TOYA: Oh—when it's so good, then it's like the good things overpowers the bad. People don't get upset when you mess up because mostly you do helpful things. That's your reputation.

MANUEL: Yeah—and they forgive you faster.

MARIA: Are there people who might not have thought Ben was good?

MANUEL: The British! We need a book that tells what they think!

What's of importance here is that one reader, Manuel, noted a lack of differing perspectives—and paused to question why. This can only happen when readers are exposed to a range of perspectives often enough, and use these perspectives to support critical efforts so that they not only come to expect the range in perspectives but they also value them as a means of building stronger understandings. The important question in this situation becomes, "Whose voice is not heard, and why?"

REVELING IN A CHALLENGE

Reading, thinking, and talking among multiple sources of information for the purpose of answering complex questions and understanding compelling issues requires specific attitudes about learning in challenging situations. As we shift from short-term "activity-based" instruction to ways of engaging in prolonged efforts toward larger goals, children need to learn to revel in a challenge. This will occur only when they believe they are capable of emerging successfully from the experience, and only if they have strategies that support them in initiating and sustaining the effort and see that the effort is worthwhile.

I was observing instruction in a fourth-grade classroom and took a moment to chat with Charlie, who was clearly struggling with his work.

CHARLIE: (Slumped in his chair) This is hard!

MARIA: What are you going to do?

CHARLIE: (Shrugs)

MARIA: What do you usually do when something seems hard?

CHARLIE: Tell the teacher.

Maria: Then what?

CHARLIE: Maybe she'll give me something easier.

Charlie does not lack intelligence and is not by nature a lazy child. Rather, Charlie lacks a belief in his own ability to tackle the work; he also lacks strategies to support his efforts, and any sense of why he should even bother to do so. As Charlie views learning, life would be simpler and much more pleasant if the teacher just erased challenges with easier assignments.

Let's visit another classroom, one which encourages and supports children in taking on challenging learning, and observe two children with very different attitudes about challenges. The children were working toward the ability to think critically about nonfiction text. I sat next to Miesha and Salvatore as they were just settling into their work for the morning.

MARIA: So what are you two thinking?

SALVATORE: It's really hard, so we don't know what we think yet.

MIESHA: But it's okay that it's hard, 'cause we know what to do.

MARIA: What do you do?

MIESHA: When it's hard, we get to really think. That's how your brain grows. Well, it doesn't really grow—you know—like the size.

SALVATORE: Yeah—it's like you just get to be a better thinker.

MARIA: So, how do you get started on something that's hard?

MIESHA: See that chart up there (pointing to a chart hanging from a stand in the front of the classroom)? It helps us to think about places in the text we need to pay attention to, and where to think harder, and it gives us questions to ask while we read.

Salvatore: Then we talk about it and think together.

Classrooms that mold such positive attitudes about challenging learning situations create individuals far better prepared to tackle complex issues in life than classrooms where children are not asked to take on challenges or supported in doing so. While a wide variety of factors combine to create this positive attitude, three stand out as fundamentally essential.

Redefining Intelligence

The first of these factors is a specific belief about what intelligence is and an awareness that intelligent behavior can actually be learned. In *Mindset: The New Psychology of Success* (2006), Carol Dweck, professor of psychology at Stanford University, outlines two mindsets, or beliefs, about intelligence. Which view of intelligence you subscribe to, Dweck asserts, profoundly affects the way you approach challenging situations. The first mindset treats intelligence as a fixed quantity, a quantity "carved in stone" (p. 6). According to this mindset, the fixed mindset, either you are smart, or not. Either you understand, or you don't. If you don't understand, well then, you're just not smart enough. Mistakes or incorrect answers are proof of inadequacy. Individuals who subscribe to this mindset become frustrated when success is not immediate. They view themselves as unable to learn, or no good at this particular task.

Conversely, there is a second mindset, the growth mindset, which conveys the belief that anything can be learned over time through passion and effort. Those who subscribe to this mindset believe in their ability to grow as thinkers. Individuals with the growth mindset understand the difference between not knowing and not knowing *yet*. To them, not trying just doesn't make sense. Mistakes don't unravel them; rather, mistakes are viewed as a part of the learning process. As David Perkins explains, learners with a growth mindset understand that "learning comes by increments; you have to hang in there and persist, winning your way to an understanding" (1992, p. 36). Miesha and Salvatore had developed this understanding, and they were not about to let their current lack of understanding immobilize them.

As teachers, we have tremendous influence in shaping children's beliefs about intelligence. When we assign challenging tasks with little strategy support, and then make those tasks easier when children struggle, we convey the message, "This is too hard for you, and you are not capable of success." However, when challenging experiences are accompanied by thoughtful strategy instruction, appropriate levels of support, and ample time to apply those strategies, we communicate a very different message to children. Our instruction clearly says, "You know what to do, you have the tools and the time, and you are capable of succeeding."

Offering reflections that directly highlight process and effort helps children "see" the route to their own success and encourages replication. When we highlight children's strategy use and celebrate their drawing upon behaviors such as persistence or flexible thinking, they connect success with effort.

Children who believe that effort leads to success are not only better situated to take on challenging learning in the classroom, but they are also poised to be lifelong learners who are confident in their ability to succeed.

Making Process and Strategies Visible

Central to the ability to persist in the face of challenging situations is a strong grasp of the process and strategies necessary to succeed. At all times, we aim high with our instruction and employ approaches and supports along the release of responsibility continuum. This careful instruction enables success and gradually builds toward independent ability, especially when it includes explicit debriefings of the process and strategies children engaged in, and offers time to reflect on their effectiveness.

An understanding of the process and the strategies used during the process enables children to plot their approach to, and their efforts through, a challenge. Without debriefings that make the thinking visible, children may be able to engage in challenging learning with teacher support, but will not be able to replicate the success when working independently or with a peer. Debriefings may be provided during or after a learning experience to sum up the constructed understanding and to unpack exactly what was done by learners to achieve that understanding. Let's listen in as Jeralyn Treas pauses midway through a read-aloud to make process and strategies visible. Her third graders were studying George Washington, searching for qualities that would define him as an American hero. They had paused to think and talk together and were ready to re-immerse in the text. Before doing so, Jeralyn wanted to be sure all children were aware of what they had just accomplished by thinking and talking together, and how.

> "So, it sounds as if we're thinking that George Washington was quite brave. This conversation started because Toya questioned George's behavior. Manuel pushed back by reminding us of the time George lived in—the way of the world back then. So, you questioned, you were flexible with your thinking, and you used an important strategy for understanding biographies—considering the person in the time that he or she lived in. Let's keep reading and see if your thinking grows or changes."

When process is slowed down and the strategies in use are studied, pausing to chart the strategies creates tracks of thinking that support children in replicating them. The chart Miesha and Salvatore pointed to as they described the way they took on a challenge was an artifact from a series of lessons debriefed for just this purpose. Strategy charts, as I describe in *Comprehension Through Conversation* (2006), capture strategies used to pursue big ideas and specific ways of thinking across multiple sources.

Figure 2.3 is a strategy chart created for a particular text, *Strong to the Hoop* by John Coy, during a fiction study of the interplay among story elements. The chart records tracks of the children's thinking inside the text. The column to the right delineates the strategies children used to construct this understanding.

The strategies distilled from the work will enable children to replicate the process—reading, think-

Expanding Comprehension With Multigenre Text Sets

ing and talking their way through fiction and biographies with lessening support as they build purposeful interdependence and strong independent abilities. The ability to construct strong understanding of a single source will help children as they work to think and talk among many sources. Over time, they will begin to detect similarities, differences, and patterns in the effect people, events, and places have on each other. These understandings, constructed by thinking and talking among multiple sources, will help children engage thoughtfully

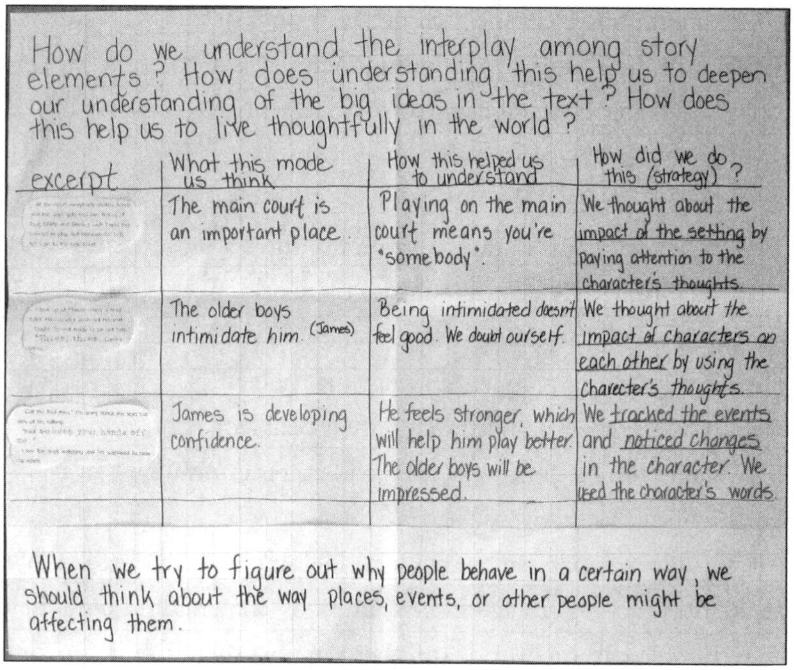

Figure 2.3: A strategy chart created for *Strong to the Hoop* by John Coy

with their world by drawing on their growing understanding of the way events, places, and other people in their world affect them, and vice versa. Strategy charts, such as the one above, will guide their efforts until habits of thinking in this way become second nature.

Viewing the Effort as Worthwhile

A belief that an intellectual struggle is worth the effort is absolutely necessary for children to continually pursue and immerse themselves in the challenge of constructing understandings of big ideas. This worth is born from the success children experience when they realize not only that they understand, but also that they can *use* what they understand to better situate themselves in their world.

Understanding, by Perkins's definition, is not just about the possession of knowledge, but about being able to use that knowledge to do something (1992). When children have read, thought, and talked among sources of information critically, they develop an awareness of the range of perspectives and opinions that surround a topic or issue, building a broader understanding. When they are able to use this knowledge as they consider their world, form their own opinions, and then act upon the world based on those opinions, they are using their knowledge generatively.

As we noted, Manuel, Alani, and Toya, immersed in their study of American heroes, began building the realization that sources of information with alternative points of view on many of the famous people they were studying were difficult to locate. This caused them to think more seriously about the power of reputation and its role in creating a legacy. The three children used this understanding to act upon their world, attempting to shape their behavior and the behavior of their peers by reminding themselves and others that their digressions might have a lasting effect. The children went so far as to create a sign, shown in Figure 2.4, which they taped to the classroom door, making sure this realization settled over them each time they headed out into the world.

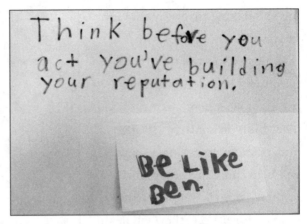

Figure 2.4: A sign created by Manuel, Alani, and Toya

In this way, the children were using knowledge generatively, creating understandings that helped them to shape their world through their behavior. This ability to take positive action made their effort worthwhile.

This doesn't happen by accident. Helping children realize that knowledge is to be used requires deliberate teaching. In all of our studies, we ask children how their developing understandings will help them live in the world, and then support them in imagining possibilities. Gradually over time, children begin not only asking this question of themselves, but expecting a meaningful answer as well.

Creating Habits of Mind

Lauren Resnick (1999) squarely states, "One's intelligence is the sum of one's habits of mind." Perkins adds to the importance of strong habits of mind, noting that, "High mental ability alone may serve us well when we're sitting at a desk, pencils poised; but good habits of mind keep us going in the rest of the world" (2008, p. xiv). Since we want our children to "keep going in the rest of the world," to find success in a world filled with complex issues and big ideas, and to become prolific thinkers, being certain they develop the necessary habits of mind becomes critical.

Strong habits are created when we engage successfully with desired behaviors repeatedly over time. When we teach children to read, think, and talk among sources of information in the pursuit of ideas, they are continuously drawing on strategies and developing attitudes and behaviors that enable them to succeed, even in challenging learning situations. They construct a vigorous sense of what it means to truly understand and develop the drive to understand and the stamina to succeed. This work must begin in kindergarten and grow in complexity each year, with children engaged in opportunities that require them to continually think strategically and refine their sense of what it really means to comprehend.

Only when habits of mind are formed can we be sure that children have truly learned how to learn—how to construct and expand comprehension on their own. For, as Nell Nodding asks (2008), "How can we claim to educate our students if they do not acquire the intellectual habits of mind associated with thinking?"

Expanding Comprehension With Multigenre Text Sets

Chapter 3

What Are Texts Sets, and Why Do We Need Them?

> I've always felt that a person's intelligence is directly reflected by the number of conflicting points of view he can entertain simultaneously on the same topic.
> ~ Abigail Adams

Spring was shifting into early summer, and my second and third graders, a remarkably independent and passionately curious group, had spread around the room, two or three to a group. They were reading, thinking, and talking among sources of information in text sets created to explore the qualities that constitute an American hero. As I was ending my first conference and considering my next, I spotted Issy, Melissa, and Brea. They were huddled on the carpet, a collection of texts about Abraham Lincoln stacked off to the side, earnestly focused on two biographies spread in front of them. The girls were gesturing from one to the other, talking furiously, yet looking confused. As I pulled up beside them, the confusion spilled out.

ISSY: Mrs. Nichols, this book says Abe had four children—see?

She was pointing to a page in *A Picture Book of Abraham Lincoln* by David A. Adler, a dump-truck-of-facts style of biography, which showed Abe and his wife surrounded by drawings of their four children.

ISSY: But this other book (pointing, head shaking side to side)—it says here—when Abe was president—it says "we took our three sons, Tad, Willie, and Robert to the White House."

"This other book," the book Issy was shaking her head at, was *Abe Lincoln Remembers* by Ann Turner, a rich, nontraditional biography crafted to create the sense of Abe Lincoln speaking directly to the reader.

BREA: Yeah—one book says four children, and the other says three.

The girls had just stumbled upon a crucial discovery that can emerge only from multiple source work. Texts may contain discrepancies in information. Not only had the girls discovered a discrepancy, but they had paused, and were reading, thinking, and talking to try to make sense out of it all. I had to dig further.

MARIA: So, what are you thinking?

BREA: Well, we think maybe this author (pointing to Ann Turner) didn't really know. But she shouldn't write a book if she doesn't really know.

MARIA: So, you think Ann Turner didn't do her research?

ALL THREE GIRLS: Yeah!

This is certainly a plausible means of explaining away the dilemma. But what the girls hadn't noticed was that one of the texts, *Abe Lincoln Remembers*, couched the information in time. What would they do, I wondered, if this were pointed out to them?

MARIA: I'm noticing something about Ann Turner's information. It says, "When I moved into the White House . . ." When was that?

MELISSA: Oh—maybe later?

BREA: Well, yeah—'cause he [Abraham Lincoln] wasn't old in this picture (pointing to a page in *A Picture Book of Abraham Lincoln*).

ISSY: So maybe it was only three children then—cuz—who was missing?—Edward—he had maybe gone somewhere?

BREA: Oh—maybe he moved to college! [After all, this is what Brea's brother had done.]

MARIA: How can you find out?

BREA: Maybe other books will tell us more?

MARIA: I'll leave you to explore this and see if you can figure out the reason for the difference in information.

I went back to my conferring, making a note to myself to check back with the girls the next day. Two conferences later, I felt a light but insistent tapping on my arm. I turned to find the girls, tears rolling down their faces, a third text in their hands.

BREA: He died, Mrs. Nichols. Edward died.

MELISSA: That's why he didn't get to go [to the White House].

Admittedly, encouraging inquiry and self-propelled learning through accessing multiple sources may not have been the best choice in this situation. Yet, the girls had strategically gone to the Civil War Era tub in the classroom library, where they found and consulted *Abraham Lincoln the Writer: A Treasury of His Greatest Speeches and Letters* by Abraham Lincoln and Harold Holzer. The book was far too challenging for them to read with depth on their own, but we had read some of the letters together, and they remembered the text had a timeline in the back. The three theorized that a timeline of Lincoln's life might offer clues as to the activities of his children. Detailed in the timeline was the date of Edward's birth—and, just shy of four years later, the date of his death.

As Brea and Melissa explained to others who gathered around, Issy, with tear streaks still on her cheeks, looked thoughtfully at the picture of Lincoln on the cover of the text, and said, "I wonder if he was sad while he was president. It would be kinda hard to be president if you're sad."

Without missing a beat, Brea looked to Issy and answered, "Well, we'll have to see if any of the books tell us. Hey, maybe that other one . . ."

And with that, the girls made a beeline back to their text set, me trailing along behind them. What they had just done was incredibly complex—they had drawn from their reading, thinking, and talking among multiple sources to construct understanding and ask a pivotal question. This process led the girls to the construction of a theory about Abe Lincoln, a theory well beyond the literal information in the texts, one that ultimately allowed them to construct a stronger understanding of Lincoln as a person. How many eminent Lincoln scholars have theorized as to Lincoln's emotional state during his presidency? Although the theories posed by these experts are far more sophisticated, with a greater range and depth of evidence as support, Issy, Brea, and Melissa were most certainly emulating the expert's process.

This depth of understanding of Abraham Lincoln occurred because this group of second and third graders were reading, thinking, and talking among multiple sources of information as a means of constructing an expanded comprehension of the sources themselves, and of the topics, issues, and ideas the sources were selected to support. The children had thoughtfully selected sources to create their own text sets, planned a progression through the sources, and were using them as a springboard for critical thinking and talking.

In *Books and Beyond: New Ways to Reach Readers* (2006), Opitz, Ford, and Zbaracki draw upon Schole's definition of intertextuality to describe the kind of work Issy, Brea, Melissa, and their classmates were engaged in as "reading both across and against texts" (p. 23). They go on to add, "If every text stands alone as an experience, the potential for critical dialogue and more sophisticated understandings is very limited."

In this instance, reading, thinking and talking among multiple sources brought to light a discrepancy that was caused by a lack of awareness of the way time framed the facts in the differing texts. But with access to a wide range of sources of information and the habit of reading with the expectation that ideas in texts may differ, children will discover and learn to think and talk about differences in information that are based on deeper divides—such as differences in author purpose and point of view. It is this level of awareness and conversations about these differences that lead to critical dialogues and more sophisticated understandings, as Opitz, Ford, and Zbaracki suggest.

As the girls headed off to explore their newly-formed theory of Lincoln, I tagged along, questions filling my head: Were they aware which genre would offer them the greatest sense of Lincoln, the person? Did their text set contain a text from this genre? Would they search for new texts to explore their theory if necessary? Would they consider searching for sources of information other than traditional text? Would they read these sources critically, considering the role of author's purpose and point of view?

Not surprisingly, the girls' ability to thoughtfully gather a variety of multiple sources and read, think, and talk among them had ample room to grow. Yet they had come incredibly far in their ability to expand comprehension by drawing on these sources.

So, what exactly are these text sets? What sources are needed to create them? And once we have a handle on what text sets are, how do we teach children to gather these sources into text sets and use them to read, think, and talk purposefully? How do we teach them to expand the understanding constructed from single texts by drawing on multiple sources? And, once children develop the ability to construct and use text sets to the extent that Issy, Brea, and Melissa have managed, how do we continually lift the level of thinking and talking among these sources, and in doing so, continually expand children's ability to understand?

The remainder of this chapter will address the essential "what" questions, first by defining text sets and then by exploring possibilities for the range of sources of information we might use. This exploration will be broken down into conversations about genres, text types, media forms, and varied levels of texts. Later, Chapter 4 will continue the conversation with a focus on the "how" questions—how do we teach children to gather and read, think, and talk their way through multiple sources of information?

Note that our conversations about multiple sources of information will require that we broaden our definition of the word "text." This term should no longer conjure an image of traditional books neatly lining library shelves. Rather, the term "text" should now refer to thoughts gathered by an author in a range of media forms, from traditional books to digital text, still shots, and video. Following suit, the term "read" becomes a reference to the interaction between the reader and an author's message, regardless of media form.

Defining Text Sets

Quite simply, text sets are a collection of sources of information that have a commonality; that is, they explore a shared topic, issue, or big idea. In the classroom, text sets become an essential tool for teaching children to gather and draw from multiple sources of information when exploring topics, issues, or ideas—they are a tool for creating what we hope will become a lifelong habit of mind.

The idea of text sets gained popularity with Richard Allington's assertion that classrooms should have books at various levels on a topic to allow all children access to content (2002). This was based on the realization that grade-level textbooks are often too complex for many of our children. As Allington has pointed out, this single-source curriculum design left many children without access to information (2001, pp. 44–45).

While supporting content instruction is certainly justification in and of itself for using text sets in the classroom, we know that multiple sources of information enable us to expand comprehension of topics, issues, and ideas in every facet of our lives. To support children in understanding the power of multiple sources and the process for using them thoughtfully, we must present text sets as a natural method of building understanding as we explore big ideas about our world beyond content instruction. Toward that end, we use text sets in the classroom as we explore big ideas in narrative studies as well as social and political issues and historical understandings, both formally and informally, throughout the day. Children engaged in the process of selecting text sets, as is the group in Figure 3.1, and then in reading, thinking and talking among them should become commonplace in our classrooms.

Figure 3.1: Children engaged in the process of selecting text sets

To support strong expansion of comprehension, text sets should include a variety of genres, text types, levels, and media forms. Most important and as much as possible, sources of information that represent multiple perspectives should be included. It is these sources that expand the conversation and, in doing so, truly expand the level of comprehension. As Laura Robb explains, "exposing children to multiple texts may result in consideration of more diverse ideas and concepts than what might occur when using single texts" (2002, p. 31).

As children grapple with the differences of opinion in texts, they struggle with questions about an author's decisions, the beliefs or points of view behind the decisions, the effect on readers, and the way the information bumps up against information from other sources. When children are immersed in this struggle over time, they begin constructing their own beliefs, and do so smartly by drawing on a strong base of well-rounded information—as opposed to being persuaded by or simply believing a single source.

Figure 3.2 illustrates a process Jeralyn Treas's third graders engaged in as they explored the issue of wolves and their reintroduction to specific regions in the U.S. The children recognized that each source of information they explored allowed the author's voice to enter into the conversation. They placed each text along a continuum of support for the wolves based on the author's point of view. Over time, as the reading, thinking, and talking among the sources allowed each child to discover his or her own point of view, each placed a sticky note with his or her name along the same continuum.

Most of the children ended up moving their sticky note several times as particular authors and the conversations about the texts built a strong case, raised new questions, or validated and strengthened previous information. This made visible not only the power of the individual sources in a text set, but

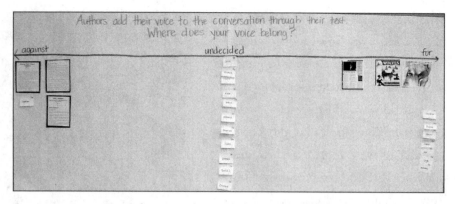

Figure 3.2: Continuum of support for wolf reintroduction in a third-grade classroom

also the power of including texts with a range of points of view. It also highlighted the necessity of the individual to think critically when faced with differing opinions, to synthesize the information, and to act on it thoughtfully.

CONSIDERING THE GENRES, TEXT TYPES, AND MEDIA FORMS NEEDED FOR STRONG TEXT SETS

Strong work with text sets begins with strong comprehension of single sources of information in a variety of genres, text types, and media forms. While genre, text type, and studies of varied media forms are not the focus of this text, what becomes clear is that children will need a balance between studies that teach the habits of mind necessary to be successful readers and writers of these sources of information, and studies of the *process* of teaching children to read, think, and talk among these sources for the purpose of constructing stronger understanding. Some of this work with genres, text types, and media forms will need to precede the use of text sets, and most certainly it will need to live alongside the work as children's use of text sets and the varied sources they comprise continues to deepen year to year.

In her exploration of genre studies, Heather Lattimer notes that, "In order to become competent, literate members of society, students must be able to navigate multiple genres" (2003, p. 3). This stance is corroborated by Margaret Mooney, who nudges us to "extend the range of materials used for demonstrating, modeling, and instructional purposes, as well as for students' use for independent reading and writing" (2001, p. 3). Mooney indicates that this is critical to support "the gamut of reading and writing experienced in daily life." (p. 3). Each genre included in text sets allows the reader to learn about the genre itself, at the same time it adds richness to the developing understanding of other sources of information, and ultimately to the topic or issue being investigated.

Differing formats also add richness to a text set. Picture books may focus on a smaller moment in time and support visualization; newspaper articles may contain many differing points of view and more current information, while feature articles in magazines often offer entertaining twists. When we read,

Expanding Comprehension With Multigenre Text Sets

think, and talk among a variety of these text types, we begin to understand more fully the ways authors choose to share thoughts about the world, the range of feelings about the topic of issue, and the way their choices shape our understanding.

Of course, media texts now permeate our world—from our computers to the Internet on our phones, video screens in the car, and infomercials at the grocery store check-out line, we are bombarded by information via varied media sources. Knowing how to "read" these texts and integrate our thoughts about and from them with the ideas we build from other texts is a crucial step in the process of constructing strong understanding of topics, issues, and ideas in our world. These media texts need to be as present as possible in our classrooms, and children must learn to think and talk about them just as they do more traditional texts.

What skills and strategies and ways of thinking do children need to truly understand the range of sources they will encounter? Do they have specific strategies to approach a text crafted as a magazine article as opposed to a picture book? What role do these same strategies and ways of thinking about texts play in understanding other media forms, such as video, photographs, television, and information posted on Web sites? Do children understand the way authors position these texts to act upon the reader? Do they appreciate the way each genre, text type, and media form adds to the richness of a text set and to the construction of understanding? And, if children truly understand, what should their talk about these sources and, ultimately, the understandings they enable sound like?

The genres, text types, and varied media forms of text included below are a quick peek at some of the sources used in text sets in the studies referenced in this book. This should in no way be considered a complete list of possibilities! Randy Bomer, in his foreword for Lattimer, notes that, as our world changes, "genres are proliferating like snowflakes in a blizzard" (2003, p. x). The same could be said for text types and media forms. What's important is that children come to realize a definition of "text" in the broadest sense of the word, and recognize that access to and critical thinking among a wide range of texts are necessary for understanding our world.

The Role of Varied Genres

JASON: It's like people, they had slaves—but we couldn't figure out why.

ERICA: We read the books—mostly they're biographies and information—and they helped us know how they (the slaves) felt. So we didn't get why other people wouldn't get it.

JASON: Yeah, so we got this book—it's the real fiction . . .

ERICA: Historical fiction . . .

JASON: Yeah, and it helped us to think more about the people then. They didn't all think there should be slaves. So we're looking for another fiction like that because they help us to get the people.

ERICA: We're gonna see if we can figure out why some of the people wanted slaves and some cared about them and said it was bad.

This snippet of conversation was part of a reading conference in a fourth-grade class exploring issues related to slavery. The classroom teacher and I had noted that Jason and Erica were expanding the range of genres in their text set, and we wondered about the thinking behind the new choices. Jason and Erica not only explained the progression of reading, thinking, and talking through their text set, but their reasons for gathering alternative choices also revealed a developing awareness of varied genres and the strength each brings to the conversation.

Authors of different genres approach a given topic or issue with varied purposes. While the author of an expository text may work to bring the reader the facts through his or her lens, a biographer will choose a key figure related to the topic or issue and argue a given stance on the individual. Authors of historical fiction and realistic fiction may attempt to paint the broader context in which all of this fits, while poets use language to paint a picture or convey an emotion—again through the lenses of their own purposes and points of view.

The table in Figure 3.3 (see pp. 39–40) focuses on the range of genres we're most apt to readily find in our classrooms. It outlines why each genre is an important addition to a text set. The table also highlights specific awarenesses that reading and thinking about the texts in one or more genres should create, and what talk indicative of strong comprehension inside this genre and among other sources of information might sound like.

The conversational possibilities used as indicators of strong comprehension in Figure 3.3 and in the tables that follow are representative of what we are aiming toward as opposed to what may be our starting point; they illustrate talk at the level of critical understanding necessary in our world today. While the children's conversation inside a specific genre and among other sources of information may not start out at the level indicated in Figure 3.3, we must remain ever mindful of the depth of comprehension we are teaching toward, and continuously nudge children toward not just becoming text participants but text users and text analysts. As we pursue this depth of understanding, we are creating a stronger basis for children's forages among multiple sources of information.

Expanding Comprehension With Multigenre Text Sets

Figure 3.3: GENRE

Genre	Purpose in text set	Awareness built when children read, think, and talk among this genre and other sources of information	What talk indicative of strong comprehension might sound like
Informational (Expository or narrative)	To gain a foundational understanding of topic or issue, or add more complex information	• Notice inclusion or exclusion of facts, and consider reasons why • Note confirmation of previously learned information, or discrepancies • Stronger sense of author's purpose • Stronger sense of author's point of view; may come to realize that there are conflicting points of view • Better able to judge reliability of information in this and other sources	• I didn't know that . . . • This information is making me wonder about . . . • The author seems to really be saying . . . (big idea) • This author seems to be trying to . . . (purpose) • The author seems to think . . . (point of view) • I think (own point of view) because . . . (evidence) • This helps to explain the information in the other source I was reading . . .
Biography	To construct a deeper understanding of key people involved in the topic or issue through a variety of perspectives	• Understand who people tend to consider the pivotal figures inside the era, topic or issue • May understand that different authors have different points of view about the person, their actions, and the outcomes of their actions	• Wow, this person seems really . . . • This author seems to think that this person . . . (point of view) • I think this person is (own point of view) because . . . (evidence) • The evidence supports/doesn't support the author's argument because . . . • The other sources I read helped me to understand why this person may have . . .
Autobiography	To construct a deeper understanding of key people through their own perspective	• Understand that the author may have a different perspective on him- or herself and the events or issues that touched his or her life than other authors do • May gain greater insights about motivation	• I think this person wrote about his/her life because . . . • This author seems to think _ about him- or herself (point of view) • I think this person is (own point of view) because . . . (evidence) • The evidence supports/doesn't support the author's argument because . . .
Realistic fiction	To introduce a point of view that supports readers in gaining a deeper understanding of people and issues that affect us all	• Stronger understanding of people and their ways of handling universal issues • Offers a point of view about people and the world to think against • Stronger understanding of what motivates people	• This helps me to understand people and their behavior because . . . • This story seems to really be about . . . (big idea) • I think the author told this story because . . . (purpose) • The author seems to think . . . (point of view) • I think the author wrote about _ (big idea) in this way because . . .

Figure 3.3: GENRE

Genre	Purpose in text set	Awareness built when children read, think, and talk among this genre and other sources of information	What talk indicative of strong comprehension might sound like
Historical fiction	To introduce a point of view that allows readers to gain a deeper understanding of people, events, the way of the world at a specific time, and the interplay between these	• Stronger understanding of the fact that people are often shaped by the time and place they live within, and vice versa • Stronger understanding of the world makes us better able to judge the point of view of biographers • Better understanding of why specific events occurred	• I know this part is fiction because . . . • The fiction parts help me to think more about the facts by . . . • I think I understand this time in the world and the way it affected people better because . . . • This author seems to be mixing fact and fiction to . . . (purpose) • This author seems to think . . . (point of view)
Primary source documents	To experience documentation that brings the original voices and spirit of the time to the conversation	• Allows children to judge information for themselves, then compare and contrast with secondary (or even further removed) source texts • Supports the understanding that secondary (and further removed) texts are often interpretations of primary sources	• This kind of text usually . . . (purpose) • I think the author was trying to . . . (purpose) • This author of this text is (sourcing) . . . • This author seems to be saying . . . (point of view) • This supports/does not support what that other source seemed to be saying . . .
Poetry	Offers a different perspective and way of treating the topic or issue	• To provide an emotional interpretation of a person, event, or issue	• This poem seems to really be about . . . • The way the author used language makes me think he/she believes . . . (point of view) • I really understand how this author feels about . . .
Propaganda	Allows opportunity for close study of the way authors within a topic or issue work to manipulate thinking	• Provides basis for compelling conversation when read against other texts	• This text is clearly trying to . . . (purpose) • I can see what the author is doing . . . • The author wants us to believe this because . . . • I read some informational sources about this, and I know . . .

The Role of Varied Text Types

JOSIE: We're studying George Washington to know why he was such a good leader.

JAMIE: We have chapter books, but we want to read some of the picture books, too.

JOSIE: Yeah, they help us to see the characters and the times because of the pictures, and sometimes they describe better. And sometimes they're just about a time in his life—not his whole life. So they tell more details, like this book is just about when he was a general.

JAMIE: And we can read more of them because they go faster, so we get different opinions from the authors.

The Role of Varied Media Forms

TIFFINY: The video is how we know that they [the Wright brothers] were really brave.

JUAN: Because we read about the first flight, but we didn't know until the video—it showed us the plane going up . . .

TIFFINY: It couldn't fly good! It bounced all up and down.

Juan: It could barely go up! When we saw it, we knew that not anybody would do that!

TIFFINY: I wouldn't do it!

JUAN: So, now we get that they didn't just have everyday braveness. They were braver than all the other people.

Juan and Tiffiny, two third graders exploring the Wright Brothers as possible contenders for the designation of American hero, were explaining the importance of a film clip of the Wright brothers' historic flight as a piece of their text set. Their teacher found the clip online, and the two students watched it over and over. As they explained, without the visual text, they had no way of understanding the depth of courage (or foolishness, depending on your point of view) required to attempt that first flight.

Today's expanding media landscape demands that we expand our instructional definition of text to include video and other visual images, online text, and text in a multitude of other media forms not traditionally used in the classroom. Each of these forms holds the capacity to expand comprehension greatly if children learn to think critically about the author's purpose, point of view, and choices.

Again, the media forms included in Figure 3.5 are those most often used with elementary age children. There are many possibilities beyond those listed, including blogs, wikis, and podcasts.

The Role of a Range of Levels in Texts

DEJANEA: Hey, there's picture books, biographies, and . . .

SAMUEL: Oh—here's Cheryl Harness. I read her books before. But they're kinda hard.

DEJANEA: I don't know much about this yet—the Revolution—so don't start with something hard. We gotta learn about it more first.

SAMUEL: So, let's start with this. It's kinda information and has lots of headings and pictures—you know—not real, 'cause they didn't have cameras then. But it'll help us learn some first.

DEJANEA: (Takes book and flips through it) Oh, you mean like drawings and maps and stuff. Yeah—that'll help.

SAMUEL: Then we need some other kinds, like historic fiction. It helps us to know the people and how the world was back then better, and get us ready for the harder books. 'Cause it [the world] was different, you know?

This conversation in Stacie Wright's fifth-grade classroom came as Samuel and Dejanea were constructing a text set from sources about the American Revolution. The class had enough texts to

Figure 3.5: MEDIA FORMS

Text type	Purpose in text set	Awareness built when children read, think, and talk among this genre and other sources of information	What talk indicative of strong comprehension might sound like
Video	Supports stronger visualization when reading, and access to details that aren't easily conveyed through written text	• Allows children to gain a stronger sense of a setting—place and/or era • May allow a glimpse of an actual person or event children would not have experienced otherwise	• Now that I've seen this, I understand better because . . . • I didn't expect this to look . . . • Now that I've seen this, the sources I've read make more sense because . . . • This author presented the information differently . . . (point of view)
Web sites	Allows children to experience a wide range of authors—those well versed on their subject and novices—with a wide range of purposes and points of view	• Awareness of a wider range of purposes and points of view • Greater awareness of the depth of interest and emotion that surround a topic or issue	• I wonder who wrote this . . . • Can we verify what this author says? • This author presented the information differently . . . (point of view) • There are so many Web sites. That must mean . . .
Photographs	Adds a visual representation of a topic or issue	• Awareness that visual images are constructed by authors with a purpose and point of view	• I wonder why the author of this image chose to show this in this way? • I think the author wants to . . . (purpose) • This image suggests that the author feels . . . (point of view) • This photograph is different from the illustrations in . . .

fill several tubs, and the two students hovered over one, musing over titles, pulling some out for closer inspection, flipping through to check complexity level, genre, and text type. Samuel and Dejanea had learned quite a bit about smart text-set selections, including the importance of starting with something manageable when tackling a new topic or issue.

The level of challenge in a text is an important consideration when constructing text sets. Laminack and Wadsworth (2006) note that a progression through a text set often begins with a text that serves as a foundation for the journey. Often children and teachers alike dismiss a text as "too easy" based on the level of the text. However, when studying topics, issues, or ideas we have little prior knowledge of, starting with a less complex text helps us begin to construct understanding, giving us entry into more complex texts. From there, the other texts can be layered on, allowing readers to continually increase their level of understanding.

Additionally, having texts on the topics and issues at a variety of levels allows struggling readers to be active participants in the construction of meaning. Children at differing levels are provided access to the reading, thinking, and talking, and through this, gain access to the process required to understand their world. When we gather the sources that children will peruse as they construct text sets, we must

Expanding Comprehension With Multigenre Text Sets

keep in mind not only the range of readers we typically have in our classrooms, but the need for all learners—ourselves included—to begin with information at a simplified level, and then build on it.

Why text sets? What becomes abundantly clear as children read, think, and talk using text sets is that consistent engagement with thoughtfully constructed text sets containing multiple sources of information expands comprehension in numerous ways, including the following:

- Providing access to a topic, issue, or idea for all children
- Bringing in the voices of a variety of authors, allowing for multiple perspectives, which form the basis for critical conversations
- Offering a variety of genres, text types, and media forms that vary in the manner in which the author approaches the topic, issue, or idea
- Developing habits of mind necessary to engage with issues and big ideas outside the classroom

Given this, how can we continue to constrain our comprehension instruction by relying on a progression of unrelated single sources? How can we define comprehension of a text as an end, rather than a means—the starting place for reading, thinking, and talking among multiple sources that will lead to an in-depth understanding of our world?

Chapter 4

The Role of Purposeful Talk in Teaching Children to Read, Think, and Talk Among Multiple Sources of Information

> Discourse doesn't make thought visible, rather thought
> is internalized discourse.
> ~ Courtney Cazden

It was a gorgeous spring morning, a Thursday, an odd day for the official end to a luxurious three-and-a-half-week break. I strolled toward Jeralyn Treas's third grade class, expecting a first-day-back slowness: groggy children wandering in late, misplaced materials, partnership confusions—the usual.

Instead, I wandered into a level of energized erudition that made me wonder if this class had indeed taken a break at all. I heard the talk as I approached their open door, more of a lively buzz than specific words. I crossed the threshold to find an animated circle of children on the carpet, well into a read-aloud of *Amelia and Eleanor Go for a Ride* by Pam Muñoz Ryan. The class was reacting to the fact that Amelia, a woman who lived at a time when women's roles were very narrowly defined, flew airplanes alone and that others thought this was, in the children's words, crazy.

Antonio: It's like Ben Franklin. People thought his ideas were crazy.

DARRION: Oh! (rising up on his knees and pointing to and reading an Albert Einstein quotation on chart paper) "For an idea that does not at first seem insane, there is no hope."

ALI: It's what we said on our American Hero chart—they had ideas that were ahead of their time. I think Amelia's like that.

KEVON: We know Amelia wouldn't stand for people telling her she couldn't fly.

TOYA: We don't know it yet, because we don't know her so well.

KEVON: Well, yeah, but I think—and we have all the other sources, so I think we're gonna find out that.

JERALYN: So, you have a theory about Amelia already, and you're going to use our text set to support this theory?

NICOLE: We need that kind of biography that people write about herself [themselves] so we know what she thought.

What's so incredible about this conversation is that the children were not only continuing ways of thinking and talking among sources of information as if there had been no interruption in instruction, but they were also referring to supports created almost a month ago as if they were newly constructed.

When children read, think, and talk among sources of information, they are building ongoing conversations that allow them to construct deeper understandings about a topic or issue. The process work we engage in with text sets—actually teaching children how to read, think, and talk among multiple sources—holds equal importance to the end product—expanded comprehension—because this understanding of process is what enables independence. This combination of using talk for the co-constructing of ideas, and using talk to focus and reflect on the process used in that construction, ensures that both the end product of that thinking—the co-constructed ideas—and the ways of thinking and talking stay with the learner, developing habits of mind.

And, as Courtney Cazden alludes to in the epigraph that opens this chapter, engaging in talk—focused, purposeful talk—allows children not only to use the rising spiral of ideas to construct stronger understanding but also to listen to the ways others think, and receive feedback on their own thinking for the purpose of strengthening their abilities. When children talk purposefully with others, they learn that there are often points of view that differ from their own, conflicting ways to interpret information, and a range of connections and opinions that may support or push against initial understandings. Gradually, they begin to search for these possibilities, expanding their understanding even when reading and thinking alone. In essence, through talk, the children are building both productive interdependence and successful independence (Nichols, 2006; Perkins, 1995). And, when the thinking and the conversations are pushed beyond the pages of a text and into the world, and are used to encourage children to imagine possibilities, the children learn a way of using their constructed understandings that is foundational to future success—their own personal success and our collective success as a democratic society.

Putting Purposeful Talk to Work

As we engage children in the process of learning to read, think, and talk among multiple sources of information, we utilize all instructional approaches along the release of responsibility continuum to form habits of mind in our learners. Modeling the use of multiple sources with think-alouds is vital, as it offers a peek inside the mind of a reader who is proficient in utilizing multiple sources of information to truly understand. Read-alouds, shared reading, and guided reading involve the children in the process of reading, thinking, and talking among multiple sources of information with gradually lessening support. And, conferring during independent reading offers immediate feedback, which children are able to use to shape their efforts and gauge their progress.

As illustrated in Figure 4.1, purposeful talk plays a foundational role during the entirety of the instruction along the release of responsibility continuum. Again, talk encourages the purposeful interdependence that enables the construction of the strongest meaning, and talk makes thinking visible, enabling children to learn patterns of thinking that move them toward successful independent efforts.

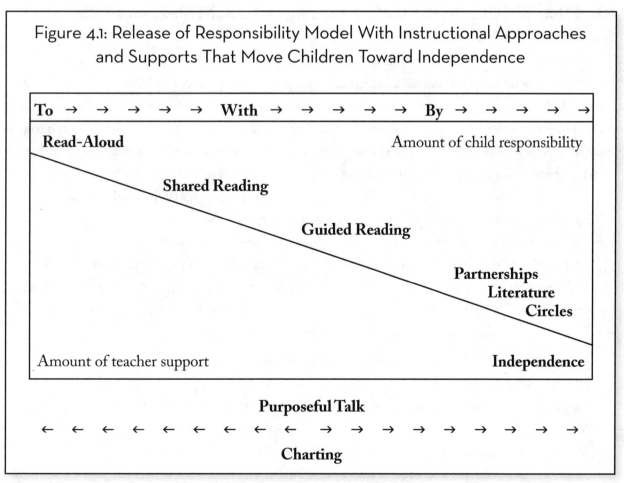

Figure 4.1: Release of Responsibility Model With Instructional Approaches and Supports That Move Children Toward Independence

Adapted From *Comprehension Through Conversation* by Maria Nichols. Heinemann, 2006.

Using talk as a social support for the construction of meaning also enables all children, including our youngest learners, to participate in the process.

FIRST STEPS: Using Talk to Understand Single Sources

Children's ability to expand comprehension by reading, thinking, and talking among multiple sources of information is predicated upon their ability to understand single sources in depth. If children are stalled at a literal level of thinking with single sources, their use of multiple sources will be bound by this same limitation.

Conversely, children who have developed the ability to tease out big ideas in texts, identify and use author's purpose and point of view to think critically, push back at ideas, and question what they read—essentially moving beyond being text participants to become text users and analysts, as discussed in Chapter 3—will bring these same abilities to their use of multiple sources. For this reason, we continue to deepen children's ability to understand all genres, text types, and media forms in and of themselves as we simultaneously teach them to read, think, and talk among them.

BEYOND SINGLE SOURCES: Learning to Read, Think, and Talk Between Two Sources

We begin nudging children from meaning bound by a single source of information to meaning expanded through multiple sources of information by teaching them to read, think, and talk between two sources. When children are new to reading, thinking, and talking between two sources, we scaffold the process by offering instructional opportunities that allow for the construction of meaning of each source separately prior to thinking and talking between the two. We start by thoughtfully selecting sources that clearly enhance each other, which will lead to a stronger understanding than either source in isolation. Then the children are engaged in instructional experiences designed to spark the level of thinking and talking that will enable them to construct understanding of each source on its own, making sure to pursue big ideas, think critically about these ideas, and use the ideas to rethink their world.

I began this work with my second and third graders using sources on topics that fascinated the children. Our first experience focused on sharks, and we launched it with *Chomp! A Book About Sharks* by Melvin Berger. The talk excerpt that follows came towards the end of the read-aloud, which was designed to construct a strong understanding of this author's big ideas.

> KENNY: It's like a lot of facts about how sharks sneak up on you.
>
> DESIREE: Not us—their prey.
>
> KENNY: We could be their prey. It's because why I only go in [to the ocean] to my knees.
>
> MANNY: But, it's not—not just facts. It's how it [the author] says it.
>
> ISSY: Oh—you mean it's like persuading—word choice!
>
> MANNY: Yeah—like the seal page. It says he [the shark] sinks the teeth in.

L.G.: (Grabbing stomach as if he were being bitten) Arghhhh!

ANTHONY: That's kinda like the title. It scares everybody.

ISSY: That's word choice, too.

MARIA: So, what does this author seem to be saying about sharks?

JAILYN: They're sneaky and scary, so watch out!

The children were using talk to co-construct an understanding of a text crafted to angle facts toward creating a sense of wariness, if not actual fear, in the reader. The next day, we dove into "Swimming with Sharks," a magazine article by Gerry Bishop, again in a read-aloud designed to support children in constructing an understanding of big ideas. The excerpt below came midway in the children's conversation about the article.

TAMARA: Saving sharks? Hey—why is he talking to us about saving sharks?

SERGIO: He said people are killing too many—but they kill us!

ANTHONY: Yeah, but he doesn't talk a lot about that.

CHENELLE: It's on purpose. He says they hardly ever kill us, but I saw it on TV— they do kill us.

ISSY: That's persuading—if it's on purpose.

TAMARA: It said about bees—because bees kill more than sharks? He wants us to be scared of bees more than sharks.

AMBER: The author had him—the diver, he's an expert— the author used him on purpose—like he thought we would just believe him!

MARIA: It sounds as if you're narrowing in on this author's purpose. What do you think his big ideas are?

MANNY: It's like he's saying people should care about sharks.

Once again, the children's ability to think and talk together led to a co-construction of understanding well beyond the literal level of the text. After the children constructed an in-depth understanding of each source of information, I launched an instructional experience designed to support them in thinking between the two books for the purpose of constructing a stronger understanding than either source in isolation would allow. This instructional experience involved the rereading of some parts of each text and asking questions designed to guide children toward expanded understanding.

I started by asking the children to rethink the big ideas in "Swimming With Sharks." We took time to ponder whether they were the same or different than the big ideas we constructed for *Chomp! A Book About Sharks.*

KENNY: The first one wanted us to know about lots of sharks. He [the author] told facts.

JAILYN: But he made the facts sort of scary.

STEPHEN: But the other one didn't just tell us facts. He told about those people who care about them, too.

MANNY: Well, yeah—that's 'cause he tried to make sharks not be scary.

ISSY: But Manny, the first book also said sharks are amazing—it was at the end.

MANNY: But he didn't try to get us to save them!

AMBER: I don't want to save them, 'cause they're scary.

MANNY: But Amber, some of us do!

(Chorus of "yeahs" for support)

MARIA: So, you've read, thought, and talked about two sources of information about sharks. Does each author have the same big ideas?

SERGIO: No—only one wants to save them.

MARIA: What does this make you think about sharks?

MANNY: Well, not everybody feels the same about them. Some are scared, and some care to save them. If you want people to get persuaded to care about them, it's hard!

ISSY: You have to persuade against the authors that tell that they're scary and just want to kill everything, and all the people who think it, too.

At first, the children's thinking and talking between sources of information hovered around comparing and contrasting literal information. Note that a little exploratory talk is what allowed the children to rise above the literal and co-construct an idea beyond what either text offered on its own. In essence, these children discovered an issue that those who work to protect sharks struggle with endlessly!

This instructional sequence stretched over three days due to the amount and depth of thinking and talking. Taking time is necessary, however, as the children have to experience this journey of thought in supportive, instructional situations, with enormous amounts of purposeful talk, in order to co-construct meaning and make thinking visible. Toward this end, a necessary step after a conversation like the one above is reflecting on the effort in order to help children to see what they had just done—co-construct an idea bigger than the ideas in either text alone—and how they had done it.

To prepare children to take on this same level of thinking and talking with greater independence, this sequence of instruction will need to be repeated many times, with a wide variety of texts and topics. With each subsequent experience, we continue to immerse ourselves in reading, thinking, and talking between texts with a broader range of sources and a greater variety of genres, text types, and media forms.

FROM TWO SOURCES TO MULTIPLE SOURCES: Teaching Children to Create a Text Set and Read, Think, and Talk Their Way Through It

Once children have developed some independent ability with reading, thinking, and talking between two sources of information, we begin the shift to thinking and talking among multiple sources of information. To support children in building toward strong independent ability with multiple sources, we include instruction in assembling text sets as we teach children to read, think, and talk among the sources.

When we teach children the thoughtful construction of a text set, we emphasize decisions based on several factors: the learner's level of prior knowledge of the topic, issue, or idea; the questions or needs driving the learning; and, of course, the use of a variety of genres, levels of text complexity, text types, and media forms. The greater the range in sources used, the better we're preparing children to handle the array of sources in the real world, and the greater the probability of encountering varied purposes and points of view to propel the thinking and talking—as we would expect in the real world.

The simultaneous teaching of the construction of a text set, and reading, thinking, and talking among the sources, begins with a multi-day instructional experience designed to support children in using that process with a teacher-selected text set around a topic or issue sure to captivate. During this first instructional process, teacher modeling will offer insight into the thinking behind the selected sources of information in the text set, and into the construction of meaning enabled by the text set.

This first instructional experience is followed by continued experiences over the course of several weeks. Each experience should draw the children increasingly into the text set selection process and encourage them to use their developing understanding of the way text level, genres, text types, and media forms work in concert to expand comprehension. Soon, children are experimenting with the creation of their own text sets, and our role shifts from modeling to coaching as we support children's decisions and efforts to utilize the sources to their maximum potential.

Teaching children to read, think, and talk inside a text set requires that not only purposeful thinking but also purposeful talk be emphasized and carefully supported. We engage children in purposeful talk not only to construct meaning but also to make the process of using a text set as visible as possible. Charting understandings during these conversations ensures children have tracks of the thinking to support their independent efforts.

When we work our way through a text set, we begin with a launch text used as a read-aloud (or supported viewing if a visual source is used). Just as we do when reading, thinking, and talking between two texts, we use purposeful talk to co-construct deep, critical understandings of the launch text. Once the children reach an inspiring depth of comprehension with the launch text, we read aloud the second source of information, working toward the same depth of comprehension. Again, as with teaching children to think between two sources, we then support children in constructing new understandings by drawing from each source. From there, children are taught to navigate the remaining sources of information, thinking and talking to understand each, then persistently revisiting each previous source and the understanding they had constructed up to that point through the lens of that new source—and all with a focus on continuously reshaping and expanding comprehension. Finally, this entire instructional experience is debriefed through the lens of the expanded comprehension, the role each source played in the construction of understanding, and the process itself.

Figure 4.2 (see p. 54) offers an outline of this instructional sequence which gradually releases responsibility to the children for selecting, and then reading, thinking, and talking their way through a text set. We'll explore the teacher's role in orchestrating whole-group instruction in greater depth below, as well as

Figure 4.2: TEACHING CHILDREN TO CREATE, READ, THINK, AND TALK THEIR WAY THROUGH A TEXT SET

	Purpose	Teacher's Role	Children's Roles
First instructional experience	This first experience is designed to introduce children to the idea that a thoughtfully selected set of sources of information in a variety of genres, text types, media forms, and levels helps us to construct a stronger understanding than single sources alone.	• The teacher shares a text set already created, discussing the topic or issue to be explored, the sources of information selected to support the learning, and the thinking behind the choices. The teacher charts the thinking as a support for future independent efforts. • The teacher uses the text set for a series of read-alouds and shared readings, supporting the children in understanding each source of information on its own and in concert with the others, and emphasizing the way each source adds to the developing understanding of the topic or issue. • The teacher supports the children in thinking and talking among the texts, debriefing and charting the process.	• The children engage in meaning-making of each source of information in the text set, and use teacher support to participate in the thinking and talking among sources of information during whole-group instruction. • Independent and partner reading continues with single sources of information and between two sources.
Second instructional experience	This experience offers children supported engagement in the process of selecting a text set from a larger collection of sources, including conversations that teach them how to plan a smart progression through the text set. The process continues to help children understand how the use of multiple sources of information expands comprehension.	• The teacher thinks aloud as he or she selects a text set from a larger collection of sources of information, involving the children in the process. The think-aloud includes considering the complexity of the texts, genres, and text types. Previous charting is used to guide the effort. • The teacher uses the text set for a series of read-alouds and shared reading, supporting children in understanding how each source adds to their developing understanding of the topic or issue. Each day, the teacher thinks aloud about which source it makes sense to read next and why, encouraging input from the children.	• The children engage in making meaning of each source of information in the text set and take greater responsibility for the thinking and talking among sources of information during whole-group instruction. • Each child meets with a partner to determine a topic or issue to pursue. • The children each select a source of information on their topic or issue. • The children read, think, and talk their way through single sources of information and between two sources. Some partners may venture into text sets and begin thinking among sources on their own.
Third instructional experience	This experience offers children the opportunity to take on greater responsibility for selecting a text set from a larger collection of sources. The experience continues to teach children how to plan a smart progression through the text set, and continues to help them understand how to think and talk among the sources to expand comprehension. In addition, the children take on the responsibility of creating their own text sets for partnership and independent reading. The teacher observes, assesses, and supports this process through conferences, workshop shares, and mini-lessons designed to address wobbles.	• The teacher continues to use text sets for whole-class instruction, sharing the decision-making with the children, and supporting meaning-making as necessary. • The teacher confers with partners, highlighting and sharing smart ways partners are selecting, progressing through, and thinking among sources of information in their text sets.	• The children engage in making meaning of each source of information in the text set and take greater responsibility for the thinking and talking among sources of information during whole-group instruction • Each child meets with a partner to determine a topic or issue to pursue. • The children work together to pull a set of approximately five sources from a larger selection, using the charts created during previous learning experiences as a support. • Partners plan progression through their sources of information, using the charts created during previous learning experiences as a support. • The children read, think, and talk their way through their text set, flowing from independent reading to partner talk about their developing understanding over the course of a week or longer.

the children's role in these experiences, using instruction from the Unit of Study suggested in Chapter 7 as it played out in Jeralyn's third-grade classroom, and excerpts of her children's talk to bring the instruction to life.

In Chapter 5, we'll come back to this chart to discuss the release of responsibility to partnerships as the children begin to take greater responsibility for this work.

First Instructional Experience: Strong Support

MARCUS: It's like George Washington's a real person, with troubles like his teeth and
everything.

ELAINA: He's a great leader *and* a regular person.

TOYA: He wasn't always perfect like we thought. It's not good that he had slaves.

LUIS: Yeah—I know it's how the world was then. But he was a leader. We know the soldiers trusted
him. But black people couldn't trust him.

MARCUS: So it's like heroes aren't always perfect. But he was an American hero. Every author—
that's their point of view. It's what most people think.

JERALYN: What do you think?

MARCUS: Maybe like eighty percent a hero?

We designed Jeralyn's first major foray into teaching her children to read, think, and talk among multiple sources as an opportunity to delve deeply into an inquiry unit that developed an understanding of American heroes. Rather than simply teaching the children about American heroes, as the third-grade California social studies standards suggest, Jeralyn and I knew the children would construct a stronger understanding of each potential candidate if they co-constructed ideas about the individuals by reading, thinking, and talking among multiple sources. A discussion of the planning of this unit of study, and the unit design itself, can be found in Chapter 6.

Through the study, which spanned five weeks, we challenged the children to define for themselves the qualities of an American hero, and then decide which of the candidates they pursued through multiple sources had what it takes to be deemed as such. This push toward determining whether individuals were American heroes helped us aim the thinking and talking beyond the literal, encouraging children to use the information they accumulated to think deeply about the qualities of each individual, and moreover to analyze not only the individuals, but the value of the sources of information they were using to construct understanding.

For this heavily supported first experience, Jeralyn preconstructed a text set about George Washington. Washington was chosen purposefully, as all the children had some baseline knowledge of him and knew he was widely believed to be an American hero. This comfort of the known allowed the children to focus more energy on the work with multiple sources and to tease out the qualities they felt earned Washington the designation of American hero—if they agreed he was indeed such a person.

George Washington by Lola M. Schaefer was chosen as the launch text simply because it was a fairly uncomplicated biography. So uncomplicated, in fact, that many of the children voiced concern right off the bat that the text was "too easy." Jeralyn convinced them to give the text a go and hold off on judging the value of the source as a part of the text set until they were deeper into the text set and their understanding of George. The read-aloud was designed to nudge children toward using the dates to consider the way of the world at the time Washington lived, and further, to use the simple facts to begin making inferences about specific qualities that Washington possessed. From this, the children were able to see the value of starting with a foundational text to gain a factual base and begin to form theories beyond the facts. They were also able to add crucial dates to a class-constructed timeline (shown in the photos in Figure 4.3) of people, events, and discoveries, which helped them consider the way of the world at specific points in time as they explored people inside this study and throughout the year.

As the class's second source, Jeralyn had selected *George Washington: First President* by Mike Venezia. The children's first inspection of the text led them to believe it was fiction due to the comic-book style of illustrations. During the read-aloud, they were surprised to find a more complex biography of Washington. This led not only to growing conversations about Washington, but also to conversations about the author's purpose, possible reasons for the style of illustration, and the need to closely scrutinize sources as we assemble text sets.

As a third source of information, we turned to a nontraditional text, the Mount Vernon Web site, for a virtual room-by-room tour of Mount Vernon. The children were stunned to find that Washington's home was treated with so much respect and care. This, they felt, told them much about the man. Their emotions ranged from breathless wonder as the visual sweeps of rooms, such as George

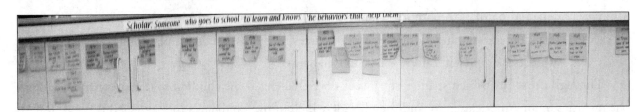

Figure 4.3: Examples of class-constructed timelines

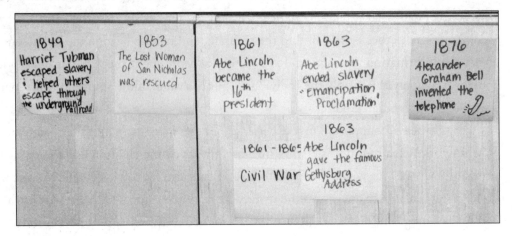

Expanding Comprehension With Multigenre Text Sets

Washington's study, revealed elegant surroundings filled with books, to stunned disbelief as they discovered that the mansion had slave quarters. As might be expected, this revelation not only became the basis for elevated levels of discussion about Washington, but left the children in a quandary as to whether he could truly be considered an American hero.

The fourth source used in the text set was *When Washington Crossed the Delaware: A Wintertime Story for Young Patriots* by Lynne Cheney. This text, filled with primary source quotes, focused on specific battles in the Revolution, bringing the war and Washington's leadership to life. While the facts in the first two sources in the text set certainly helped the children to construct meaning, it was actually the virtual tour of Mount Vernon that best helped the children to make sense of not only the difficulty of battle, but also the character of Washington himself. As Kenya finally came to see it, "If he left Mount Vernon to do this, it [the colonist's desire for freedom] must have been really strong in his heart."

For our fifth source of information, we stayed with a traditional text and used *George Washington* by Cheryl Harness. This biography is a far cry from the simple source which launched the study. It took all of the understandings the children had constructed together, and knowledge gained from the student partnerships that had begun to explore other sources of information about Washington in their partner and independent reading, to construct meaning. This experience enabled the children to think and talk with greater depth not only about Washington but also about the progression of work through the text set—about the importance of beginning with more supportive sources, then moving to more complex sources as understanding grows.

On a whim, we added a last source to this text set—*George Washington's Teeth* by Deborah Chandra and Madeleine Comora. We felt this choice was important in that the text is a fictionalized account of George's struggle with his teeth. The text served many purposes. First, it taught children that real information can be mined from many different types of texts. It was a step in highlighting the value of using facts rather than just acquiring them, as the children had to put factual information from other sources to work to understand unexplained references. The text also opened the door to further conversations about the way of the world at the time George lived, which were essential to understanding Washington as a person. Although fictionalized, the children came to understand this source's value in the text set. As Marcus so eloquently said, "Without this book, I couldn't know that George Washington's a real person with problems just like everybody!"

By the end of the text set, the children were keenly aware that their understanding of Washington had expanded far beyond the level the first two sources alone enabled. They understood Washington as a complex person with struggles and faults, but also as a leader with a clear vision and strong beliefs. In addition, the children were beginning to theorize about qualities that defined an American hero and were eager to dive into another text set to see if a new candidate displayed any of the same characteristics. Many children began selecting more than two texts for their partner and independent reading, although we had not yet suggested they do so.

Second Instructional Experience: Lessening the Support

KEVON: He's [Ben Franklin's] a scholar and an American hero.

HERMAN: A complete scholar.

JERALYN: What do you mean?

KEVON: He's an inventor, a politician, he loved to read, he loved music, he helped people . . .

This big idea about Ben Franklin developed over many days of reading, thinking, and talking through a co-constructed text set. The children chose Benjamin Franklin as the focus of their second instructional experience because they had heard of him, and they felt knowing more would allow them to test their theories about the qualities that constitute an American hero. This time, Jeralyn drew the children into the construction of the text set by offering a quick discussion about available sources, thinking aloud about each through the lenses of genre, text type and complexity, and the possible role it might play in the construction of understanding. The children weighed in with their own thoughts, and together they negotiated choices, admittedly nudged a bit by Jeralyn.

Drawing on their experience with the George Washington text set, the class chose *Benjamin Franklin* by Phillip Abraham as a launch text, because they recognized that this was a less complex biography. Such a biography helped them form a base of information on which to build when they studied Washington, and the children theorized that this would be a smart move again.

From there, the children (again, with strong support from Jeralyn) added *Benjamin Franklin: A Man of Many Talents* by Time For Kids. The children recognized that this was a lengthier and slightly more complex biography, and knew from experience that they would be able to build on their understanding from their first source.

As a third source, the group chose *The Ben Show*, an online video clip from ushistory.org of an actor portraying Ben Franklin and sharing what might possibly be Franklin's thoughts about the Internet were he alive today. Jeralyn and I knew this source would truly challenge the children, but we were eager to give them the opportunity to think and talk their way to understanding.

Another nontraditional text, *Ben Franklin: Scientist and Inventor*, a cartoon video from the Animated Heroes series, was selected as a fourth source of information. Again, we knew the mix of fact and fiction would offer challenges, but nontraditional sources of information are our reality, and children must learn to make sense of and use every source to its fullest potential.

As a fifth choice, the children began to look at sources that were initially bypassed because they just seemed "too hard." With Jeralyn's encouraging push, and their experience from their last text set, the children began to discuss whether, at this point in their progression of study, they would know enough about Ben to tackle something more challenging. They settled on *How Ben Franklin Stole the Lightning* by Rosalyn Schanzer, noting that they could adjust their choice if necessary.

As the children thought and talked their way through this text set, Jeralyn and I charted their process and the resulting thinking in several different ways, for the purpose of supporting the independent efforts soon to follow. The first chart provided a representation of the power of multiple sources, visually highlighting the way thinking grew with each source in the text set. To emphasize the source-by-source construction of understanding, this chart—pictured in progressive stages as the children's work with each source is unpacked in the coming paragraphs (see Figures 4.5, 4.6, and 4.7)—was color-coded by source. The chart not only supported conversations about Ben's qualifications as an American hero, but also served as a visual reminder of the progression of thinking that should unfold as the children worked independently or with partners.

Figure 4.4 offers a glimpse of a second chart under construction. This chart, which focused on the text set itself, was constructed as children read, thought, and talked their way through the set. It documented details about each source and the way each added to the developing understanding of Ben Franklin. This chart offered support as children took on the challenge of creating their own text sets.

A third chart was constructed over the duration of the entire unit, documenting the qualities the children felt defined an American hero. It's interesting to note that the first qualities added to the chart were the result of studying individuals. Over time, however, the children began to consider the people they were studying collectively, comparing and contrasting, synthesizing, and forming new understandings of qualities common to all. Again, it is thinking and talking purposefully together that made these overarching understandings possible. This chart is pictured near the end of this chapter (Figure 4.8).

Let's delve a little deeper into the progression of thinking and talking with each of these sources in the newly constructed Benjamin Franklin text set. When the children read, thought, and talked about their first source, *Benjamin Franklin* by Phillip Abraham, their conversation centered on placing Franklin in time. They used what they already knew about this period from studying George Washington plus the facts in this new text to begin considering Franklin's probable role in the Revolution and theorizing about his qualities as an individual.

As with the study of George Washington, a second more complex biography, *Benjamin Franklin: A*

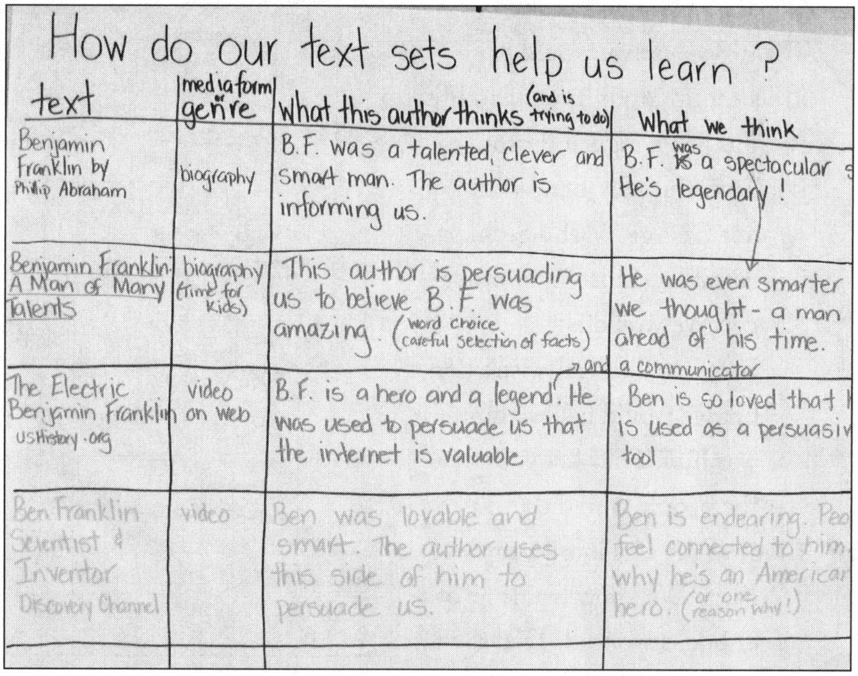

Figure 4.4: A text chart under construction

Man of Many Talents, helped the children as they theorized about Franklin. The conversation excerpt below erupted midway through the reading.

LUIS: So he's a scholar, inventive, and clever.

ALYSSA: Yeah—things can't pop in your head like that unless you're clever!

KEVON: They didn't just pop in his head—it's 'cause he's a scholar—he learned all the time.

DARRION: I think it's why he called himself Silence when he wrote. He was silent because he's always thinking.

ANTONIO: And printing was the perfect place for him because he could spout new ideas.

Figure 4.5 shows the constructed understandings of Benjamin Franklin from these first two sources of information.

As we suspected, the children's third source of information, the video clip *The Ben Show* from the Electric Benjamin Franklin Web site at ushistory.org, proved to be a challenge for the children.

LAURENA: That's him?

JADA: (pointing to the classroom timeline) Wait . . . no . . . it can't be him—look at the timeline!

ANTONIO: It's somebody dressed like him! Talking about the Internet.

JERALYN: Why would the authors of this message have someone dress like Ben Franklin?

TOYA: Because we would pay attention to it more than if it was just a regular person.

JERALYN: But why Ben? Why not George Washington, or Abraham Lincoln, or other—

KEVON: We would believe Ben—well, it really isn't Ben, but we would believe him if it was him. They know that— the people who did this.

ELAINA: And he loved people to learn. We know from the other books we read. That's what it is about the Internet—how we can learn!

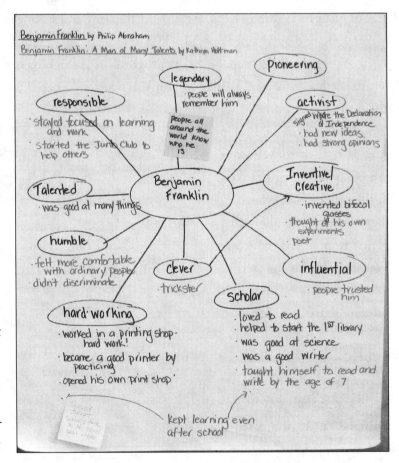

Figure 4.5: Constructed understandings of Benjamin Franklin with two sources of information

JERALYN: Even though this isn't really Ben, did we learn anything new about him from this video clip?

KEVON: Because people admire him and they know we do, too, they use him to persuade.

Figure 4.6 reveals the new ideas about Ben Franklin the children constructed through this third source of information and the integration of these understandings with the understandings constructed from the previous sources.

As you might imagine would be necessary, the children's first viewing of their fourth source of information, the video *Ben Franklin: Scientist and Inventor*, was simply for enjoyment. The children were able to confirm facts ("Oh—we read that!") as they viewed, but they did not imme-

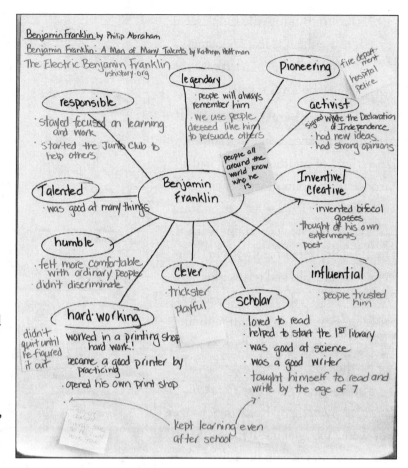

Figure 4.6: New ideas children discovered about Ben Franklin through the third source

diately or spontaneously push back at fictionalized or uncorroborated information. A second viewing framed with a conversation about watching for details that were confirmed by other sources we've read and identifying information this author is presenting that we have not yet heard from any other source enabled the children to begin to actually use the video as a source of information.

ELAINA: The magician was playing with electricity, too. Maybe Ben wasn't the only one who knew about it.

KENYA: But Ben studied it. He was a scholar.

ELAINA: Is he [the magician] real?

JERALYN: We don't know if all the characters are real.

LAURENA: Oh! It has facts and stuff that's not real. It's like that kind of book—historical fiction. It's a historical fiction cartoon!

HERMAN: It's real 'cause it showed how he loved science, 'cause his books were piled up, and his kite was in the corner.

ANTONIO: But his wife didn't seem real—she was like annoying. Ben would be married to someone who loves science.

As the conversation continued, the children realized that this author, like authors of traditional texts, had a purpose and a point of view. The video was crafted in such a way as to endear Franklin to the viewer—and it worked. The children were unanimous in their feelings of kinship and respect for Franklin. Jeralyn declared a "historical crush" on Ben, helping children to understand the power of this media form!

By the time the children reached their fifth source, *How Ben Franklin Stole the Lightning* by Rosalyn Schanzer, they were talking about Ben as if he were a true presence in their lives. They understood the impact he had on our world today, from both the text set and

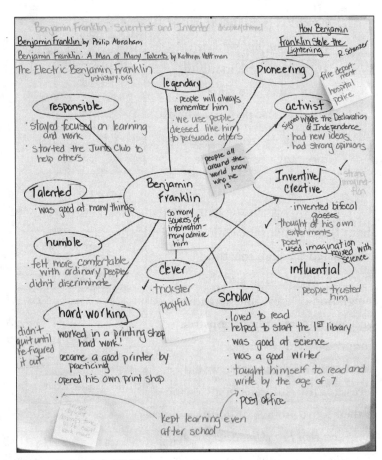

Figure 4.7: The children's constructed understandings of Ben Franklin through the 5th source of information.

understandings shared by groups of children who were scouring other sources of information about Franklin on their own. A photo of the children's constructed understandings of Franklin is shown above (Figure 4.7). This is not the final version, as partners who continued the study of Franklin on their own continued to add to the chart. As the snippet of conversation that opened this section suggests, the children believed Franklin to be a truly unique individual who drew from a wealth of talents to shape his world in positive ways.

Third Instructional Experience: The Children Take Greater Control

Amelia Earhart was selected as the third individual in the American heroes study. Jeralyn made this suggestion to the children in order to include a woman and move the conversation about heroes into a different era. As Jeralyn described the possible sources, she allowed the children greater latitude in drawing on their understandings from the previous instructional experiences to create the text set.

This text set was more varied in terms of text type and modes and levels of information simply because of the range of sources available online. With some support, the children selected these sources:

Expanding Comprehension With Multigenre Text Sets

- *Amelia Earhart* by Wil Mara (easy biography as the launch text)
- *Amelia Earhart* by Marilyn Rosenthal and Daniel Freeman (slightly more complex biography)
- Page four in *Amelia to Zora: Twenty-Six Women Who Changed the World* by Cynthia Chin-Lee (vignette)
- *Amelia Earhart* (video clip from YouTube)
- Article from the July 3, 1937, *New York Times Magazine*
- *Amelia and Eleanor Go for a Ride* by Pam Muñoz Ryan (historical fiction)

The children's willingness to tackle such a wide range of sources, and their confidence in their ability to construct meaning with them, offered a wonderful barometer of progress. While a good deal of support was needed with many of the more varied media forms, the children's determination and willingness to be risk-takers with exploratory talk enabled success not only in terms of the constructed understanding of Amelia but also in their understanding of the importance of constructing meaning using a wide range of varied sources of information.

WHERE TO FROM HERE?

After these experiences, which also included work with a fourth text set on Dr. Martin Luther King, Jr., the children's understanding of an American hero, shown in Figure 4.8, had grown to encompass many qualities. They noticed that certain attributes were evident across all or many of the individuals they were studying. Their own conversations began to foster not only introspection about what each attribute really meant but also a comparison of the degrees of each attribute in these heroes, in famous people we often read about today, and in themselves. The following excerpt is typical of their conversations about American heroes.

JERALYN: What is the difference between being famous and being an American hero?

KEVON: A hero has to do with change. He has to make a positive change on the world.

TOYA: Or *she*! Like Amelia Earhart.

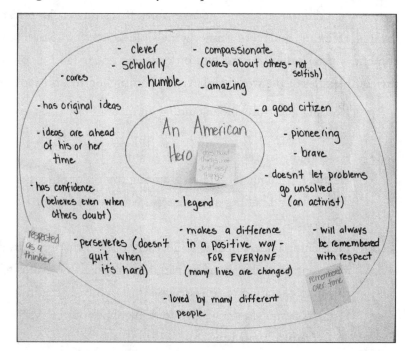

Figure 4.8: The children's constructed understanding of an American Hero at this point in the unit.

ALANI: Some famous people don't do positive change. Like rappers.

HERMAN: No! Not all of them!

TOYA: But some of them. They're not like Martin Luther King. He stood up to people for positive change.

STEPHEN: To be brave, you have to stand up no matter what and trust your heart.

KEVON: That's what changes the world.

JERALYN: So, can you change the world?

ANTONIO: Yeah—we don't have to be famous like rappers. We just have to have—like those (pointing to the qualities chart). It says "Are you a hero?" We can be if we make positive change.

After working through text sets on George Washington, Benjamin Franklin, Amelia Earhart, and Dr. Martin Luther King, Jr., supporting children in their own fledgling studies of equally notable individuals, and contemplating their understanding of an American hero, Jeralyn and I realized we had not immersed the children in a study of anyone who put their defined qualities of an American hero to the test. To challenge their understandings, we took an additional week at the end of the five-week study and worked with the children to construct a text set of Blackbeard. Most knew of Blackbeard as a movie character. Few realized he was a real person, and they were intrigued by how much and yet, how little, is known about him. The children brilliantly synthesized his qualities into the counter-category of American villain and began searching the library hoping to discover other sinister characters who might fall into the same realm.

So what did the children take away from this study of American heroes infused with instruction in reading, thinking, and talking among multiple sources? The outcome was a rich integration of literacy content, social studies content, and process—an understanding of how to learn, how to make sense of the complexities of the world and expand comprehension through the following means:

- Reading and truly understanding an increasingly diverse range of genres, text types, and media forms
- Assembling sources of information into text sets
- Reading, thinking, and talking among multiple sources of information
- Thinking and talking in purposeful ways while learning collaboratively—a critical twenty-first century skill
- Deepening understanding of a variety of historic figures and the concept of hero
- Thinking critically about individuals that society elevates to the status of "famous," and using this understanding to consider the importance of the individual
- Using constructed knowledge to think about our own actions, our place in the world, and our ability to affect our world

Additionally, the children learned to propel themselves as learners, creating a sense of exhilaration around the learning.

Foundational to all that was accomplished was *purposeful talk*. The more the children talked about the individuals in each study and about American heroes as a collective, the more they understood. The more they understood, the greater their success as they tackled increasingly complex sources—and the greater their desire to do so. And the more the children talked about process—how to construct thoughtful text sets and read, think, and talk among the sources—the greater the control they had over their own learning.

The combined effect was becoming a contagious frenzy. The children were developing what Peter Johnston refers to as "agency"—an awareness of and belief in their ability as learners (2004). Now the challenge became one of continually deepening all of these abilities. This brings us back to instruction along the release of responsibility continuum, the continued use of purposeful talk to grow thinking stronger through collaborative efforts, and to make process visible—all of which launches us into Chapter 5.

Chapter 5

Building Independence With Reading, Thinking, and Talking Among Multiple Sources of Information

> Reading furnishes the mind only with materials for
> knowledge; it is thinking that makes what we read ours.
> ~ John Locke

It's mid-morning, and Jeralyn and I are leaning against the built-in desk in the back of her classroom, surveying the ongoing independent portion of the reading workshop. Despite the label of "independent reading time," the room is not shrouded in hushed library-like silence. Rather, there is a buzz of purposefulness, the hum of a productive environment. Two children are sorting through sources of information in the Space Exploration book tub, engaged in an escalating conversation about why certain sources are more powerful, and therefore more necessary in their text set, than others.

Partnerships, deep in conversation, are seated at the children's round tables and the kidney-shaped, small-group table. One partnership is working to organize information on a chart much like the ones co-constructed during whole-group lessons. Two partnerships have a range of sources scattered in front of them, pointing to one, rereading a portion of another, flipping through a third to find a reference to some bit of needed information. Another two partnerships, both studying the same individual, have spontaneously merged into a foursome, and are eagerly sharing insights. A set of partners sits at the computer, intently studying an online video clip Jeralyn found to add to their text set. The music of these partnership conversations rises and falls with their level of intensity, and I'm struggling to decide which to eavesdrop on first.

Additionally, a handful of children are scattered around the carpet reading on their own, blissfully buoyed by pillows and kid-size rocking chairs that seem to glide in rhythm with the pace of the eyes darting across the page. Several of these children are within whispering distance of their partner, and they lean over frequently to share an eye-popping tidbit or a photograph or two. A quick chat erupts, then just as quickly, the partners settle back into their own sources, often with a renewed sense of purpose.

Jeralyn and I exchange a quick glance. We know better than to think we can luxuriate in the scene unfolding before us, as there is much work yet to be done. But for the moment, there is a sense of quiet satisfaction; a shared awareness of what these children are poised to become.

As children engage in their pursuit of expanded comprehension, taking time as teachers to observe, listen, and engage in conversations about their process and their developing understandings offers us great insight into their progress. This is assessment in its purest form: paying close attention to our learners as a means of gaining information. This information then allows us to coach on the spot and focus our lesson design so that it continues to build independence and the habits of mind necessary to be successfully literate in the world today.

Defining Independence

As teachers, we continually contemplate our children's ability to work independently. But what exactly is our vision of independent learning, and what are the behavioral traits this vision leads us to cultivate? All too often, it seems, physical behaviors top the list of desirable independent traits, with manifestations of quietness shaping the most desired behaviors. The child sits still. He or she is not up, moving about the room. He or she is "on-task"—not talking or bothering others. An assigned product is completed within predetermined time boundaries.

What this vision fails to consider is the behaviors, both physical and cognitive, that characterize our real-world learning when we work toward understanding complex issues. When faced with intellectual challenges, most of us are anything but silent and still. We talk purposefully with those in the know and those who will listen and help us sort out our thinking. We actively search for sources of information and enlist others to help locate them. Because we value the social construction of knowledge, we entice others to tackle those sources with us. We revel in the realization that thinking and talking is growing bigger ideas, taking us beyond our initial expectation, even when our preconceived time frame has to be adjusted. At times, we may appear silent on the outside. However, in our heads, battles rage as we engage in a cognitive struggle to let go of old constructs and adjust to new insights. As we emerge from the struggle, we share our new understandings with others and use their feedback to revise and solidify our thinking. Yes, these efforts are collaborative, but they are also illustrations of independence. The independence lies in our drive to know, the organization of our efforts, and our pursuit of success. These behaviors, both physical and cognitive, are truly the hallmarks of independent learning.

Consider again the changing work place as discussed in Chapter 1. In this new arena, the ability to work independently is revered. As IDEO's employees are assigned to those flexible project-specific "hot teams," certainly there is an expectation of independent ability. But what is the vision of this independence? Sit in your seat and work quietly? Stay "on-task"? Produce in isolation? On the contrary, independent ability in this arena has little to do with working alone and silently. Rather, the term **independent** is used to describe a person's ability to organize and manage his or her own process for attaining specified results. This process entails a range of abilities, including securing sources of information and initiating and maintaining purposeful interactions with the team, most often in the form of conversations, for the purpose of innovation and problem solving.

In *The Process-Centered School*, Arthur Costa and Rosemarie Liebmann (1997) suggest that schools meeting the needs of tomorrow's workplace must focus on developing an array of characteristics in their children related to independent success, including (p. vvii):

- Thinking skills
- Active construction of knowledge
- Self-assessment
- Cooperative problem solving

Although this is a challenging mandate regardless of the social configuration of the learning environment, these characteristics most certainly will not develop when blocks of time devoted to building independent ability are envisioned as time solely for reading and thinking in isolation. Becoming a strong thinker, constructing understanding and making decisions about our own progress toward understanding, and working with others to problem solve requires an active learning environment in which talk and cooperative efforts are valued and practiced.

As we consider transferring responsibility for reading, thinking, and talking among multiple sources of information to the children for the purpose of developing independent abilities and habits of mind, we must consider our vision for the block of time we label as independent practice. We must ask ourselves whether children are indeed being allowed to take on these ways of thinking and talking to expand comprehension in a student-centered, socially energized learning environment that enables the development of the characteristics suggested by Costa and Liebmann.

When our vision for independent practice is in keeping with the characteristics necessary to develop a strong ability to read, think, and talk among multiple sources of information, old norms for the independent block of time no longer apply. The children will not necessarily remain seated. Quiet will not rule the room. As in Jeralyn's classroom, children who are assuming increased responsibility for reading, thinking, and talking among sources of information may be in various stages of all three—some reading, some thinking, and some talking—at any given time. This, however, is not an invitation for chaos. Rather, it is an opportunity for us to teach children to take control of a way of learning that matches what we've been modeling, and matches the world they are hurtling toward.

Continually Propelling Children's Ability to Read, Think, and Talk Among Multiple Sources of Information

Once our vision of independent practice assures that we will be cultivating behaviors that will truly support children's efforts to read, think, and talk among sources of information, we need to focus on the instruction that encourages the transfer of the behaviors from learning opportunities led by the teacher to learning opportunities that are student-controlled.

RELEASING RESPONSIBILITY FOR THE SELECTION OF TEXT SETS

Prior to the start of our American hero study, Jeralyn's children had some experience with text sets and the work of reading, thinking, and talking among multiple sources of information. They had worked together as a class studying topics of interest and had been supported in thinking between two sources and among multiple sources. Most partnerships readily began thinking and talking between two sources, and many ventured into multiple sources. The text sets these brave trailblazers constructed were wobbly at best—often drawing from a single genre and traditional text, with little thought to the progression through the texts. But, they were a start!

In preparation for our unit, and with Jeralyn's support, the children worked to organize their classroom library into tubs of sources of information sorted according to the subject (in this case, people) of those sources. As you may have guessed, this sorting was driven by the biographies from the nonfiction section of the library. Once the biographies were sorted, the children added informational texts about the era the specific person lived in, and situations and events that related to the person. Jeralyn and I added historical fiction and realistic fiction texts we knew would support the children's efforts to expand comprehension. And, we began collecting sources from other media forms—magazine and newspaper articles, photographs, specific Web sites, anything we could find to add a greater range to the sources of information children would have available.

As we began the American hero unit, we engaged the children in instruction carefully designed to model the construction of and thoughtful progression through text sets. We knew the first text sets children constructed for their partnership and independent reading would continue to be wobbly, but we also knew they would offer feedback for designing further instruction on gathering multiple sources for reading, thinking, and talking to expand comprehension.

During the second whole-class foray into a text set inside the unit, a text set on Benjamin Franklin, we charted the sources as we progressed through each one, knowing that this chart (see Chapter 4, Figure 4.2, p. 54) would support children in the construction of their next text sets. The chart emphasized the importance of a thoughtfully selected launch text; the variety in text level, text type, and media forms among the selected sources; and the way the sources worked together to propel us into conversations that expanded our understanding of Ben Franklin, his importance in our world, and the way we were able to use his life to reflect on our own.

Chapter 4 described the process used to teach the selection of text sets. As the children took on the challenge, conferring into their efforts and sharing important understandings became pivotal to success. During their efforts to construct their second text sets, I fell in step with Nicole and Darrion, who were making a beeline for the George Washington book tub. It seems these two had decided to revisit George to learn more. Let's listen in as they get started constructing a text set.

> NICOLE: We probably don't need the easy source to start 'cause we already read one.
>
> DARRION: Yeah—I want to read that one in there that's about him and Benjamin Franklin. I saw it in here. I think probably they knew each other 'cause they lived at the same time. Here—see (holding up a copy of *John, Paul, George & Ben* by Lane Smith)?
>
> NICOLE: Who's John and Paul?
>
> DARRION: Well—I don't know. We gotta read. Hey—there's two of them! You can read it, too.
>
> NICOLE: What kind of book is this?
>
> DARRION: Well—it's real people—at least George and Ben. So probably biography.
>
> NICOLE: Is there one of those books—like history fiction—so we can learn more about the world then and how people were? We should ask Ms. Treas if we can read the Web site again, too. Because we didn't see his whole house. We can learn more about him if we study his house.

This quick bit of conversation reveals a great deal about these two children's understanding of sources of information, text sets, and learning in general. First, both Nicole and Darrion recognize that by sticking with a topic and digging further they can expand their learning. They know the value of revisiting sources, and Darrion remembered pre-scouted sources that interested him. The two are not perplexed by unknowns, but rather trust their ability to figure things out (*Who are John and Paul?*) as they go. They may not yet be adept at sizing texts up by genre, or know the exact label of all the genres, but they are aware of the variety of text genres and have some expectation of each on its own and in concert with other sources. They have not only considered the one source beyond traditional texts that they are aware of, but seem to value the range it brings to the text set and the depth of thinking and talking it generates. Sharing this with others is a reminder that success is within their reach! Future conferences will need to nudge them toward applying these understandings to an individual they don't know as well.

Antonio and Kevon were my next stop, as they had settled on reading, thinking, and talking about Henry Ford and seemed puzzled over one source in the tub. The boys had already piled up *Henry Ford* by Wil Mara (an easy biography), *Henry Ford* by Jonatha A. Brown, from the Weekly Reader People We Should Know Series (slightly more complex biography), and *Eat My Dust: Henry Ford's First Race* by Monica Kulling (historical fiction) on the carpet. They were huddled over *Henry Ford Museum: An ABC of American Innovation*. As I sat down next to them, their confusion spilled out.

KEVON: Mrs. Nichols, we don't get this book.

ANTONIO: It says Henry Ford, and it has a car here (on the cover), but on the inside it's all kinds of stuff.

MARIA: What else does the title say besides Henry Ford?

ANTONIO: Oh—that other word? It's mu . . . mu . . . mus . . .

KEVON: Museum. It's a museum. Like where they have old stuff to see. Oh! Maybe his car is there!

ANTONIO: Look! Is it there?

MARIA: Do you think this book will be a good choice for your text set?

Both boys look at each other, and Kevon shrugs.

ANTONIO: Well, it could . . . but, well . . . maybe we need a video. Wait—look at the timeline. When was Henry Ford? Was there video invented?

KEVON: (Looking in Wil Mara's biography) 1863! That's when he was born.

ANTONIO: No—not yet (walking back from the timeline, shaking his head).

KEVON: What sources do we have so far? I don't think the museum book. We gotta learn more about how he invented the car so we can figure out if he changed the world in positive ways. (He looks through books in pile.) Maybe there's a Web site. (Looking at me) Can we go see?

MARIA: Why do you think a Web site will make your text set stronger?

KEVON: Well, it could be like George Washington's and show what his house was like and what the cars were like. It would be about his world.

So how are Antonio and Kevon doing with the construction of their text set? They are definitely questioning the value of sources rather than just settling for anything. While I disagreed with their decision about the museum text, I knew there would be plenty of time to revisit its value as a source of information in a later conference, once they knew a little more about Ford. What's worth sharing with others is the boys' use of the resources at their disposal to help them determine what types of sources might be available and their efforts and willingness to expand beyond traditional texts.

As partnerships finalized their text sets, many began deciding who would tackle which source first. At this point, I found myself drawn to Kenya and Stephen, who seemed to be having an extended conversation about this. Both wanted to begin with the source they had determined would be their launch text, as they were focusing on Neil Armstrong, and neither knew much about him. We returned to the tub of sources to find that, while there was not a duplicate copy of this text, a second fairly simple biography was available. It was thus discovered that, if two fairly simple launch texts are available, it makes sense to add both to the text set so each reader has a smooth entry into the learning. A workshop share was born! This share earned "Ohs!" and "Ahs!" from the crowd for its simple brilliance. Many partnerships asked for a few extra minutes to return to the tubs of sources to see if a second text suitable for launch might be added to their text set in preparation for their work the next day.

As challenging work goes, this round of creating text sets was pleasantly smooth. But, it truly was just a beginning. Jeralyn and I spent the week conferring with partnerships, with a focus on their selected sources of information. To be sure, we found partnerships with sources that were too challenging, text sets that did not offer breadth in genre or text type, and even partnerships studying a person they had little interest in, making it difficult to sustain the effort. With each situation, we prompted the partners to think through their choices and make adjustments, using talk to make both the difficulties with their choices and the remedies visible. We checked back with these partnerships on subsequent days, making the results of their adjusted choices visible as well.

This attention to text sets continued throughout this study and the remainder of the year. Instruction in text sets ranged from supporting individuals or partnerships to providing whole-group mini-lessons when we realized a class-wide need. As you may have noted, the majority of sources of information in the tubs were traditional texts in a range of genres and text types and levels, with a mix of newspaper articles when available. Helping these third graders to add breadth to their text sets through varied media forms admittedly took some effort on our part. Jeralyn and I found ourselves making note of whom or what the children were studying, and supporting them with Internet searches for sources such as newspaper articles, video clips, and Web sites. While many of these sources were a little complex for children to understand fully on their own, the availability of traditional sources of information in varied levels offered some access. And, knowing that awareness and exposure in a supportive academic setting are crucial first steps toward becoming learners who seek out a range of sources and are adept at making meaning in all, we encouraged children to use these sources to the fullest extent possible.

THE ROLE OF PARTNERSHIPS

Throughout this and the previous chapter, partnerships have dominated the conversation. Partnerships continue to offer children the opportunity to work collaboratively with others during independent blocks of time. Partnerships (and at times groups of three or four) require that the children not only continue growing in the ability to think and talk purposefully with others but also take responsibility for the relationship and the learning behaviors and conversations that enable successful experiences.

Jeralyn and I designed her independent reading time so that partners met with each other at the start of the block to plan their work for that day. When partners first began to meet during this time, we encouraged them to plan for concrete aspects of the work that were fairly easy to control, such as which sources they were going to tackle first, how far they thought they would get in their reading, and when they might need to meet to think and talk together. Eventually, we began supporting partners in starting their work together by having conversations that involved taking stock of where they were in their understanding of their topic, issue, or idea, and then planning for what they hoped to accomplish in terms of understanding that day. That way, whether searching for sources, reading on their own, or engaging in conversation, their work was focused and purposeful.

Once their brief meeting was over, partners acted on their plan. This meant each child was not only reading and thinking to construct meaning but also taking steps to hold onto their thinking to share with their partner at the end of the independent reading time. This meant using sticky notes or reading notebooks to jot down their thoughts.

The block of time then ended with partners debriefing with each other, taking stock of their understandings to that point and reflecting on their process. To add continued learning beyond the classroom, many teachers who've taken on this work have partners make plans for home reading. The children then take their sources of information home and continue their reading and thinking. In these classrooms, the pre-conversation the next day then becomes partially a sharing of any new insights that were sparked as each partner read and thought on his or her own the evening before.

As a side note, whenever possible, we had duplicate copies of texts in the tubs so partners were able to read the same text simultaneously. But when limited resources have to be stretched, duplication is axed in favor of greater variety. Most often, this means the children are thinking and talking about the same topic, issue, or idea, but through the lenses of different sources. Learning to orchestrate these conversations took us on a whole new line of focused mini-lessons, as well.

When children transfer ways of thinking and talking to partnerships, they are taking on work that has previously been heavily supported by the teacher. Even during shared and guided reading, the teacher supports the effort by asking questions to spark conversation and by orchestrating the talk to focus and sustain the conversation. Without this support, we found many partnerships' conversations deteriorated into comparing facts among their sources. This made clear the need for ongoing lessons designed to develop the children's ability to focus on big ideas and sustain their own talk.

We knew that we would need to take more time to unpack our conversations, to make visible the types of things we were discussing and the way ideas escalated. This, along with a continued sharpening of critical thinking, became one of the foci for instruction aimed at turning greater responsibility over to the children.

PROGRESSION OF INSTRUCTION ALONG THE RELEASE OF RESPONSIBILITY CONTINUUM

As we discussed in Chapter 4, teaching children to read, think, and talk among multiple sources of information for the purpose of expanding comprehension begins with modeling. However, if it also ends with modeling, children will not learn to engage in this process on their own. Right from the beginning, we invite the children to share the responsibility for the thinking and talking during read-alouds, asking children to engage in the construction of meaning as we offer heavy support by reading the texts, planning the pauses for conversation, designing the questions, and orchestrating the talk. But if we want reading, thinking, and talking among multiple sources of information to develop as a habit of mind, the children need insight into many of the decisions we make during a read-aloud so they are able to replicate these decisions and take control of the process on their own.

Shared Reading

During shared reading, we're able to turn the texts around so the children have visual access to the text. We can slow down the process of understanding and use talk to make decisions and ways of thinking and talking about the source of information visible to children. This work most often focuses on using comprehension strategies for stronger construction of meaning and to support children in thinking with a critical edge.

It stands to reason that when we progress from reading, thinking, and talking between single sources or two sources to reading, thinking, and talking among multiple sources, partnerships would need support in elevating and sustaining the level of their talk. Shared reading also offers the opportunity to make visible the process of building strong conversations that expand comprehension with multiple sources.

We begin this process by choosing one source to revisit during shared reading, reminding the children of the way this source propelled the thinking and talking about the topic, idea, or issue. We display the portion of the text we want children to focus on using an overhead or document camera, or perhaps we cue the video clip back to the crucial spot, and ask the children to consider the way this portion of the text affected their thinking. We ask the children to reread for the purpose of figuring out exactly what sparked that specific thinking. We allow time for children to turn and talk with their partner as we listen in. Finally, we debrief by having partners share what specific place in the text (or video clip) got them thinking, and what understandings the thinking and talking led them to.

Then we go through the process with a second source, talking not only about that specific text but also about the way our constructed understanding bumps up against the thinking from the previous source of information. We again focus the children on a particular segment of the text to reread and then to think and talk about the role this specific section played in the conversation. We repeat this process with a third source, so that the children are revisiting a previous conversation with a heightened awareness of the way specific segments of each source fed into the larger conversation that developed over time.

The portions of texts we focus children on may include a rich description, a section that reveals an author's point of view, information that conflicts with other sources, and so on. Our goal is to help children develop a sense of what to be on the lookout for as they read and where to pause in their reading or revisit text to think and talk for the purpose of propelling their own conversations as we do when orchestrating read-alouds. To support children in orchestrating their own conversations, charts such as the one pictured in Figure 5.1, constructed while Jeralyn's children read, thought, and talked their way through a text set about Amelia Earhart, are invaluable.

Note that this chart focuses not only on what the class thought and talked about but also on the way doing so shifted the conversation, helping children to develop an awareness of the twists and turns conversations among multiple sources might take. Obviously, this type of charting needs to be generated from many conversations as the twists and turns the talk takes will vary in each conversation. With multiple charts as guides, there will be greater range and variations in the supports children are using to shape their independent efforts with purposeful talk. Over time, conversation about literal aspects of the texts should fade as partnerships gain greater control over ways to shape their talk using pivotal understandings from their sources.

How do text sets help us to construct bigger ideas?

source	What was important to think and talk about?	How did this grow our ideas?
Amelia Earhart by Wil Mara, biography	Basic information - dates, places	We constructed a sense of who Amelia was and what the world was like when she lived
Amelia Earhart by Marilyn Rosenthal & David Freeman	We focused on Amelia as a person - how she interacted with other people and the world	We understand Amelia better. We know she wanted wondrous lives for all women. We realized how brave she was
Amelia to Zura... Twenty-five Women Who Changed the World by Kyo Maclear	We discussed the quote - what did her words say about her as a person?	We heard determination and passion. We think that is what earned her the honor of being in this book
Amelia Earhart 1897-1937 YouTube video	We talked about the differences we could see - clothes, and the planes. We saw the way people responded to her.	We understand the depth of her bravery (those planes look scary)! We have a better feel for how famous she was.
Miss Earhart Forced Down at Sea... article in New York Times Magazine	We questioned why an article was written about her, and noticed how many theories there were about what happened.	We're starting to understand what an important person she was & how much impact she had on others. We think this is why she's so famous today.
Amelia and Eleanor Go For A Ride by Pam Muñoz Ryan, historical fiction	We focused on the interactions between the two characters.	We think being brave enough to be daring and different might be really hard and lonely even though it seems glamorous. You have to be very brave to face the world and dare to be different, and it helps to have a friend.

Figure 5.1: A chart constructed by Jeralyn's class while they read, talked, and thought their way through a text set about Amelia Earhart

Guided Reading

Guided reading, a small-group approach by definition, is also used to further children's ability to read, think, and talk among sources of information. In guided reading, children with a similar need and similar reading levels are grouped for a series of lessons designed to address that specific need. However, guided reading that focuses on strengthening children's ability to read, think, and talk among multiple sources differs in that a series of lessons designed around a single text are replaced by a series of lessons utilizing sources of information linked as members of a text set.

As with traditional guided reading, the teacher's role shifts to that of coach as she coaxes the children to draw from the wealth of skills and strategies they are on the verge of controlling. The children, though, are using those skills and strategies to pursue big ideas across all the sources rather than inside any single one in isolation. Previous sources are kept available as children take on each new one, enabling them to return to those sources to support their thinking and talking.

Using guided reading in this way ensures that children are receiving instruction in skills and strategies right at a point of need while they strengthen their ability to navigate multiple resources purposefully. This small-group format is also an excellent time to strengthen talk behavior, as the smaller group size encourages greater participation, particularly for our quieter or shy children.

Conferring

As Carl Anderson reminds us in his timeless book, *How's It Going? A Practical Guide to Conferring With Student Writers* (2000), conferences are conversations (2000, p. 6). Of course, Anderson's work concentrated on the writing conference, but the same most certainly applies for reading conferences. Immersing ourselves in a conversation is an ideal way to assess (something we'll visit toward the end of this chapter), and it's the ideal arena to nudge children—individuals and partnerships alike—toward their next steps with multiple sources.

During our conferring conversations, we listen for evidence of strong comprehension of single sources, for orchestration of the thinking and talking among the sources, and for the children's ability to use their thinking and talking to explore big ideas. Whenever possible, we lift the level of the thinking and talking, propelling the individual or partnership slightly beyond the level of comprehension they are inching towards on their own.

We also make note of the construction of text sets, the interactions between partners, and the ways the children are keeping track of their thinking (charting, sticky notes, etc.). Always, we debrief the conference, committing the children to continued effort toward what we just taught, and asking them to explain their mission in their own words. Often, these conferences become fodder for shared reading or mini-lessons, as we recognize a need for similar conversations with other class members.

THE IMPORTANCE OF MINI-LESSONS

Quick mini-lessons, drawing attention to an aspect of the work that children need to focus on as they head off to read, think, and talk among multiple sources, help propel the children toward greater success with independent efforts. Mini-lessons may focus on a variety of needs, and may range from a single lesson to a string of lessons as you dig into a need over time.

Comprehension mini-lessons may quickly refocus children on charts constructed during shared reading that support them with making meaning of single sources, or reading, thinking, and talking among sources. We remind children of the ways these charts support their efforts and help them envision using the charts. The mini-lesson offers an opportunity for partners to think using the chart as a warm-up, creating a greater likelihood that they will continue to think and talk in this way as they head off to read.

Children often need quick warm-ups and reminders to work toward continually lifting the level of their talk. Again, mini-lessons offer an opportunity to practice using charting as a support. Basic talk behavior, such as being sure all voices are heard, growing ideas, disagreeing in respectful ways, and negotiating meaning, certainly needs revisiting from time to time.

Other aspects of partnership work may require mini-lessons as well. Planning, making decisions together, agreeing and disagreeing, problem solving, and persevering can be tough going, even for adults. Children need opportunities to revisit the purpose of partnerships and to practice thoughtful ways of learning together.

You may note a need for organizational mini-lessons if children are struggling with keeping track of notes and ideas. The need for procedural mini-lessons pops up at times, as children become careless or wasteful with materials. We remind children of such things as how to store their sources day to day, how to put away sources thoughtfully (knowing another learner may need that very source), and how to make the most of every sticky note.

These mini-lessons are crucial for helping to maintain a focus on and continually rotating through the many angles of the work that need attention. Combined with instruction that supports the selection of sources of information, building and sustaining strong conversations, and working toward truly understanding, children develop the ability to independently engage in and monitor the behaviors necessary for success in and beyond the classroom.

Chapter 6

Designing Units of Study

> Make no little plans; they have no magic to stir men's blood and probably will themselves not be realized. Make big plans; aim high in hope and work, remembering that a noble, logical diagram once recorded will not die.
> ~ Daniel H. Burnham

Recently, I had the pleasure of spending a luxurious hour browsing through a local bookstore, searching for unique text to propel thinking in an upcoming workshop. My quest sent me wandering down aisles of books I usually pass by, and I soon found myself thumbing through a text by baseball great Yogi Berra (2001). As I scanned the table of contents, a particular chapter caught my eye. The title was a simple statement: "If you don't know where you're going, you might not get there." Intrigued, I flipped to the chapter, and quickly found myself drawn into the life of a person who clearly understood the importance of realizing and relentlessly pursuing goals. Yogi's goal—playing major league baseball—was set early on, and he planned and worked to make his passion a reality. Knowing what you want in life, Yogi insisted, helps.

In his off-the-cuff, accidental way, Yogi had landed squarely on the impetus behind our own thoughtful curriculum planning. If we don't know where we're going (translation: if we don't have a strong understanding of what our children need to know and be able to do) we might not get there. Stephen Covey, widely cited for his popularization of the process of backward design, takes a more strategic approach to the same understanding. As with Yogi, he points to the importance of beginning with the end in mind as a tool for building a purposeful life (1990).

In *Understanding by Design* (1998), Grant Wiggins and Jay McTighe tie the process of backward design to curriculum planning. These authors remind us that strong curriculum design does not begin with favorite books or themed activities. Rather, our work is strongest when we use the resources and research available and our beliefs about what children need to know and be able to do to form long-term goals, and plan our curriculum and instructional design according to these goals. Essentially, Berra, Covey, and Wiggins and McTighe are all saying the same thing: Developing goals and persistently pursuing them with a thoughtfully conceived course of action matters.

What We're Aiming Toward

While our work in curriculum design is clearly guided by standards, our large, overarching goals for our children are not limited to the standards. Rather, our goals wrap the content we derive from standards in attitudes and behaviors we believe are foundational to learning for the purpose of propelling children toward success in the world. To support the creation of these goals, we have available as resources a wide array of standards documents produced by individual states, think tanks, and national educational organizations. Each of these documents outlines what its particular authors believe children at certain developmental or grade levels should know and be able to do. As critical readers and thinkers, we understand that each of these documents is written from a certain perspective—specific beliefs about teaching and learning and the goals our children should reach. Knowing this, it is our responsibility to live what we preach, which means that we must read, think, and talk among an array of standards documents to ensure we develop a rich sense of possibility while keeping our eye on our larger goals: the attitudes and behaviors necessary for success. These attitudes and behaviors, including the building of purposeful talk behaviors, a focus on inquiry, the use of multiple sources of information, and the development of perseverance, help us expand our goals beyond a body of acquired knowledge to the continuous process of acquiring and using knowledge.

Developing Units for a Thinking Curriculum

Once our overarching goals for our school year are crafted, once we know where we are going, we can begin the work of figuring out how to get there. In the reading workshop, we begin by breaking our yearlong goals into smaller units, or studies. Our instructional foci for these studies may range from reading process work to developing strong abilities with comprehension strategies, genre-specific understandings of the way texts work, and critical thinking. In addition, we use the reading workshop to develop the specific attitudes and behaviors that strengthen and support learning and help build independent abilities.

As suggested by the premise of backward design, each unit is planned with the end in mind. What do we hope children will know and be able to do? Where are the children in their abilities now? How will we assess their progress along the way?

To illustrate this process, we're going to follow the development of a third-grade unit of study, an inquiry already partially explored in this text. This inquiry, titled "What Is an American Hero?" focuses on strengthening children's ability to read, think, and talk among multiple sources of information while simultaneously strengthening reading comprehension and critical thinking strategies and constructing a knowledge base to support social studies instruction.

DRAWING FROM LITERACY STANDARDS

The way in which standards are conceived and crafted varies by author. Some standards, such as the California state standards, are focused on content. Content standards are formatted as lists of specifics that need to be covered. Other documents focus less on specific content and instead are written with a broader focus, setting goals and offering a glimpse of classrooms immersed in the process of achieving those goals. These standards, often referred to as performance standards, describe the end result of rich instruction that aims high. In *How to Align Literacy Instruction, Assessments, and Standards and Achieve Results You NEVER Dreamed Possible* (2004), author Nancy Akhavan points out that performance standards are most supportive in helping us set goals and imagine achieving those goals.

Knowing this range of offerings exists in standards documents, I worked with the third-grade teachers at Webster to draw a variety of these sources in designing our yearlong curriculum and each unit inside this yearlong plan. The range of literacy standards documents used included the following:

- Standards for the English Language Arts. 1996. The International Reading Association and The National Council of Teachers of English.
- Reading and Writing Grade by Grade: Primary Literacy Standards for Kindergarten Through Third Grade. The New Standards Primary Literacy Committee for the National Center on Education and the Economy and the University of Pittsburgh.
- Mid-continent Research for Education and Learning (McREL) http://www.mcrel.org/compendium/browse.asp
- English Language Arts Content Standards for California Public Schools Kindergarten Through Grade Twelve. 1997. Sacramento, CA: California Department of Education.

Again, we crafted this unit with its major emphasis on further developing the children's ability to read, think, and talk among multiple sources of information. However, as children were strengthening this ability, we knew we needed to continue to support other aspects of their developing literacy abilities. We added to the unit an emphasis on critical thinking, including determining and using author's purpose and point of view. This decision was based on our beliefs about what it means to truly understand, as well as a clear sense of where children were with this ability, based on our ongoing assessments, not on California standards. Curiously, critical thinking is not emphasized in the third-grade standards in California—a seemingly tell-tale omission given the current condition of political and financial affairs in the state, and the desperate need at the top reaches of government for individuals who are able to able to read, think, and talk in ways that lead to innovative practices.

INTEGRATING BIG IDEAS FROM OTHER CONTENT AREAS

Like many teachers across the United States, we struggle not only with carving out time in the instructional day to teach content areas such as science and social studies, but with the well-documented depth of content versus breadth of content issue, as well. Standards documents, particularly those angled toward content specifics as opposed to big ideas, outline so much to teach that we feel pushed towards coverage, even when it is in direct conflict with our beliefs about what it means to know and understand. Textbooks and dense informational nonfiction texts certainly don't help, as they lean toward a surface-level coverage of large spans of information. Very small chunks of text are apt to contain incredible amounts of factual information with no elaboration or context to support the reader in making sense of it all. The quick pace of the crafting of these texts results in a glossing over of pivotal decisions, moments in time, and large-scale changes, rushing the reader past information that's necessary to grasp an overarching understanding of big ideas.

In *Reality Checks: Teaching Reading Comprehension With Nonfiction K-5* (2006), Tony Stead reminds us that children's comprehension of nonfiction, which would include texts used in content instruction, must move beyond fact recall to evaluative understandings (p. 114). These evaluative understandings include thinking like a text user and text analyst, as discussed in Chapter 2.

A small piece of resolving this issue is slowing the process down by allowing our students more time to read, think, and talk among well-crafted texts which support content area instruction. This allows children time to build both a foundational understanding of the content and a deep, evaluative understandings of ideas. If we fill our classroom libraries with a range of rich sources of information that support content area instruction, our literacy block can be an additional time during the day when children are offered in-depth immersion in information and ideas that support content area instruction.

Text sets, as we've discussed, allow children to read, think, and talk among multiple sources of information on specific topics or issues. If children are involved in studies with text sets designed to build strong literacy abilities while in pursuit of ideas related to content, the result is stronger understanding in both arenas. As children are building strength as readers, writers, listeners, speakers, and thinkers, they are simultaneously constructing content knowledge and understanding. While the pursuit of topics and ideas of their own interest should certainly be honored, it does makes sense to look to standards and to draw reading from the content areas into the literacy block.

A first step as we consider bringing other content into the literacy block is looking toward the big ideas in our content and finding those ideas that can be supported by a wealth of easily available sources of information. If drawing together a rich array of texts in many genres and media forms at appropriate levels is not a possibility, then it will be difficult to engage children in an inquiry that will support them in developing foundational knowledge, an understanding of big ideas, and strong meaning-making abilities.

When other content is integrated into the reading workshop, it is crucial that the lure of content not be allowed to overshadow the literacy work. Each lesson, workshop share, and other learning situation must be debriefed through meaning (the building of strong content understanding) and the process and ways of thinking and talking about texts used to construct meaning (the literacy focus).

TURNING STANDARDS INTO INQUIRY

In classrooms where teaching and learning are more passive and teacher centered, a teacher might tell children all about American heroes, or have them read brief vignettes in their textbooks. But there are at least two flaws in this plan. First, it assumes a single, correct point of view. If we want our children to develop the capacity to judge character and make wise decisions about people, shouldn't we teach them to do just this? Why wouldn't we offer our children access to all possible sources of information and allow them to decide what an American hero is and who qualifies? Second, in such an environment, instead of constructing deep understandings, information is passively received and thus, if remembered at all, rarely functions richly in children's lives.

More traditional teaching can be turned into a quest to understand and to use this understanding to build new knowledge simply by redesigning the learning as a series of inquiry questions that move from **having** knowledge to **using** knowledge. The following three questions, which build on each other and move from knowledge to use of knowledge, served to focus the "What Is An American Hero?" study.

- What is an American hero?
- How do American heroes, past and present, shape our world?
- Can I become an American hero?

The first question pushes children toward defining the qualities that separate these individuals from others. The second question nudges children to consider the effects of these differences. And, the third question asks children to consider their own lives and the people they hope to become, and to envision possibilities for themselves, both now and in years to come.

Let's consider the difference in outcome for instruction designed to tell as opposed to instruction reshaped as inquiry. In a classroom with instruction designed to tell, we would expect children to be able to list the people deemed by the textbook or the teacher to be American heroes, recite a few facts pertinent to the people's lives, and perhaps retell why others thought these people were important.

Now, let's listen in as Jeralyn's children, immersed in inquiry, discuss their developing understanding of what a hero, and specifically an American hero, is. You'll hear echoes of previous conversation as the children continue to construct understanding.

JERALYN: We've talked a lot about the qualities that heroes have, and wrote them on our chart. We thought and talked about who is and who isn't a hero, and why. Many of you think the person you are studying is a hero. Alani and Priscilla think Helen Keller is a hero. Darrion and Marcus think Henry Ford is an American hero.

DARRION: No—a world hero. He changed the whole world.

JERALYN: Ah—a world hero! But we haven't really defined a hero. What are you thinking? What is a hero?

ANTONIO: He's like someone who makes a difference in a positive way.

LAURENA: Not just "he." Girls can be heroes, too. Like Helen Keller is.

LUIS: They have to make a difference for all the people. Like they have an invention—

DARRION: Or solve problems. They don't let things go wrong. They try to fix it.

STEPHEN: That's helpful—like how Martin Luther King was. If he didn't say we should all get along, the world would be different.

TOYA: They get famous, but they don't care.

STEPHEN: No—it's not famous like rappers. Rappers are all about clothes and money.

JERALYN: Is there a difference between being famous and being a hero?

ANTONIO: To be a hero, you have to watch your actions.

DARRION: And make positive change for the world. Or for America. That's an American hero. They made America special, like Ben Franklin did, so we can be here and in school. And American heroes and even regular heroes have to be brave to stand up to people.

ALI: Yeah—stand up and no matter what, trust their heart.

STEPHEN: And have confidence to persuade us like Martin Luther King.

JERALYN: Can you be a hero?

STEPHEN: No—well, not like Martin Luther King. He told lots of people—persuaded them—

LUIS: But yeah—we can—look, Stephen—we can—like remember when, at lunch, those kids were—they were acting bad—

ELAINA: Oh, yeah, and Darrion, he persuaded them—

STEPHEN: Oh—so Darrion's a hero. Like a Webster hero!

Through inquiry, these children have constructed with great clarity the qualities that define a hero, the characteristics of certain American heroes (as well as a Webster hero), and the ways those qualities and characteristics come together to create people who rise above the norm. This is crucial, as the status of hero is in the eye of the beholder. One person's hero may be another's villain. Rather than absorbing another's point of view as passive learners, the children are developing the depth of knowledge required to judge for themselves.

The social studies content knowledge that the children construct in this literacy unit—a complex understanding of the concept of an American hero and a more focused understanding of the way heroes shaped and continue to shape America and the world—will support them as they continue to explore our system of government, and as they consider their role in the world. The knowledge will serve them well in all of their efforts to understand and create a strong sense of the type of people they hope to become.

Note that as this unit was designed for literacy instruction, an inquiry question that focuses on the process of reading, thinking, and talking among multiple sources of information was included. This inquiry question ("How does reading, thinking, and talking among multiple sources of information help me understand?") is the focus of the literacy instruction and supports children in reflecting on their progress with this ability and understanding its power. This helps ensure that children will draw on this process to succeed with any future inquiries they might create for themselves.

DEEPENING THE WORK

Let's take a moment to revisit Issy, Brea, and Melissa's work in constructing an understanding of Abraham Lincoln, which launched Chapter 3. When I came upon the girls, they were in the throes of trying to make sense out of a seeming discrepancy in information about Abe's children. Their efforts to resolve this took them on a journey of thought that led to a deeper theory about Abe as a person. Though impressive, their efforts had ample room to grow.

If you revisit the girls' conversation (see pp. 31–32), you will note that their understanding of Lincoln was constructed using traditional texts exclusively and, to the point of our conversation, all within a single genre—biography. They were comparing and contrasting literal information, which allowed them to note a discrepancy, and they were making inferences, but were not showing signs of thinking critically beyond this. Clearly, Issy, Brea, and Melissa's next steps must include learning the power of reading, thinking, and talking among a mix of genres and media forms, and pushing back critically at what they read.

What is notable, however, is that Issy, Brea, and Melissa were on the verge of shifting their talk from a topic (Lincoln) to an issue (Lincoln's emotional state and its effect on his presidency). The pivotal role talk played in this process was clearly evident, as it was the swirling elevation of ideas that shifted the girls' focus toward this issue.

This is crucial, as it is only when children are able to shift their focus from topics and facts about the topics to complex issues or ideas that they rise above literal understandings and begin to grapple with thinking that is bigger and bolder than any single source would lead them to. When children learn to use multiple sources to engage with complex ideas, they are learning how to approach a world filled with issues that aren't easily solved.

There is not necessarily a set, absolute linear progression for supporting children in shifting from topics to issues and ideas. When children are familiar with and passionate about a topic, they are often already aware of many of the issues inside the topic, as well as the varying points of view that surround the issue. Our kindergartners, with all of five years of experience under their belts, know that, when it comes to pets, there are differing opinions about what animals make good pets, who should have one, and when. Many of the children are even well versed in the reasoning behind the opinions. Conversely, when taking on learning in a new arena, as were Tanya and Sheralyn (the two girls we met in Chapter 2, sitting with their pile of reptile books trying to just make up a question), we need time to explore and learn a little before issues and bigger ideas begin to emerge.

In our modeling of reading, thinking, and talking among multiple sources of information, we must angle toward issues and ideas inside the topics we are exploring and make this process of shifting from topics to issues and ideas visible to children. Then, as we converse with children about their reading and thinking, we must guide them toward bigger ideas and issues, watch closely and provide support when needed, and highlight this so that others might emulate it.

Developing the Unit Overview for "What Is an American Hero?"

The unit overview of "What Is an American Hero?" is shown in Figure 6.1. The overview includes essential questions, goals, pivotal instruction, sources of information, and the talk we hope to hear from our children.

Figure 6.1: READING UNIT OF INQUIRY WHAT IS AN AMERICAN HERO: GRADE 3					
Essential questions	• What is an American Hero? • How do American heroes, past and present, shape our world? • Can I become an American hero? • How does reading, thinking, and talking among multiple sources of information help us to understand?				
Desired results	• Evidence of ongoing strengthening of the children's ability to read, think, and talk among sources of information in a range of text types, genres, and media forms • Evidence of an ability to determine an author's purpose and point of view, and use this information as a springboard for thinking and conversations with a critical edge • Evidence of a developing awareness of the qualities that define one as a hero, the role of heroes in our nation and our world, and our own ability to act heroically				
What to teach	**Why**	**Instructional approach**	**Sources of information**	**What might talk indicative of strong comprehension sound like?**	**What might talk indicative of strong reading, thinking, and talking among sources sound like?**
Creating text sets	Children need support in selecting a range of sources on a topic, and understanding how this range of sources expands comprehension.	Model the selection of texts, and think out loud about thoughtful progression through texts.	**George Washington:** • *George Washington* by Lola M. Schafer • *George Washington: First President* by Mike Venezia • Mount Vernon Web site (www.mount vernon.org) • *When Washington Crossed the Delaware: A Wintertime Story for Young Patriots* by Lynne Cheney • *George Washington* by Cheryl Harness • *George Washington's Teeth* by Deborah Chandra and Madeleine Comora *continued*		• *I want to think more about ___, so I'll need books that are . . .* • *I better start with a basic/easy book because I don't know much about . . .* • *I'll need some biographies because I'm learning about a person, and some informational texts to give me more details.* • *I think this is historical fiction—or maybe realistic fiction. That will help me to learn more about the world back then.*

Figure 6.1: READING UNIT OF INQUIRY
WHAT IS AN AMERICAN HERO: GRADE 3

What to teach	Why	Instructional approach	Sources of information	What might talk indicative of strong comprehension sound like?	What might talk indicative of strong reading, thinking, and talking among sources sound like?
Under-standing each source deeply on its own	Children need to think and talk about each source, pushing to-wards critical understand-ings. Readers then need to integrate this information with their own beliefs and un-derstandings to strengthen or challenge them, and con-tinue to ask questions.	Combination of read-aloud and shared reading with purposeful talk to build strong com-prehension of each text and study the strategy used as readers to construct strong meaning	**Benjamin Franklin:** • *Benjamin Franklin* by Phillip Abraham • *Benjamin Franklin: Man of Many Talents,* Time for Kids • *The Ben Show* (a film clip) on The Electric Benjamin Franklin (Web site at ushistory.org) • *Benjamin Franklin: Scientist and Inventor* (Animated Hero Classic) • *How Ben Franklin Stole the Lightning* by Rosalyn Schanzer **Amelia Earhart:** • *Amelia Earhart* by Wil Mara • *Amelia Earhart* by Marilyn Rosenthal and Daniel Freeman	• This fact makes me realize . . . . • This part is the author's opinion. It tells me that this author really thinks . . . • So this author is really saying that . . . • I think he/she is trying to inform/persuade/en-tertain, and that's why he/she included . . . • This author's ideas make me think . . . • Before I read this, I thought . . . • Now I'm more sure of . . . • Now, I'm wondering . . . • I think this person is/isn't a hero because . . . • I think all heroes are . . . because . . .	• Now that I'm learning more about this person, I think I need a source of information that . . . • The authors of all of these sources have the same point of view. I won-der if I can find an author who has a different point of view. • I'm noticing that the texts I'm finding are all (biography, informational, traditional texts, etc.). I wonder if I can find a dif-ferent (genre, text type, media form) to help with my thinking. • This video clip really changes the picture in my head because . . .
Reading, thinking, and talking among texts	Once a single source is understood, it needs to be held up to other sources. Children need to engage in thinking and talking with a critical edge. Do the facts match? Are the author's big ideas the same? Why or why not? Do the authors have the same purpose and point of view?	Modeled and shared reading with purposeful talk	• *Amelia to Zora: Twenty-Six Woman Who Changed the World* by Cynthia Chin-Lee (page 4) • Amelia Earhart 1897–1937 (http://www.youtube.com/ • "Miss Earhart Forced Down at Sea, Howland Isle Fears; Coast Guard Begins Search," *The New York Times Magazine,* Saturday, July 3, 1937 • *Amelia and Eleanor Go for a Ride* by Pam Muñoz Ryan *continued*	• At this point, all of my reading, thinking, and conversations with oth-ers have me thinking . . . • I think I will read/reread __ because I'm now wondering . . .	*continued*

Figure 6.1: READING UNIT OF INQUIRY
WHAT IS AN AMERICAN HERO: GRADE 3

What to teach	Why	Instructional approach	Sources of information	What might talk indicative of strong comprehension sound like?	What might talk indicative of strong reading, thinking, and talking among sources sound like?
Continually constructing a stronger understanding, and developing my own point of view.	As readers think and talk about a range of sources, they continuously construct and shape stronger critical understandings. Little by little the readers begin to form their own point of view.	Modeled and shared reading with purposeful talk	**Dr. Martin Luther King:** • *I've Seen the Promised Land: The Life of Dr. Martin Luther King, Jr.* by Walter Dean Myers • *Life in the Time of Rosa Parks and the Civil Rights Movement* by Terri Degezelle • *Freedom Summer* by Deborah Wiles • Text of "I Have A Dream" speech (portions)	• Now that I've read many sources and talked with others, I'm beginning to think . . . • At first I thought . . . I still think . . . or Now I'm beginning to change my thinking because . . .	
Using this information to live smartly in the world	Knowledge is power if we use it in thoughtful ways. Children often need support in using what they know to generate new knowledge and shape their world.	Thinking and talking together, and modeling ways of using knowledge	• Video of "I Have a Dream" speech (portions) http://www.youtube.com/watch?y=iEMXaTkUfA&feature=related ch?v=dAP91BnYlm4)	• Now that I know heroes ___ , I think I should . . . (action) • I want to tell _ to try to inform/persuade/ entertain him or her because . . . • Others should be interested in this because . . .	• Reading, thinking and talking among all of these sources really helped me because . . . • I've been wondering about . . . Now I know I need to read more sources and think and talk with more people to figure it out.

KNOW WHERE YOU'RE GOING

Again, to be true to the heart of backward design, we must have a firm grasp of the desired result of our instruction for each unit we design over the course of the year. When we are clear about what we hope the children will achieve, we are able to stay continuously alert for signs of progress along the way, and to provide support effectively. Our desired end results, or goals, for "What Is An American Hero?" are listed below.

• Evidence of ongoing strengthening of the children's ability to read, think, and talk among sources of information in a range of text types, genres, and media forms

- Evidence of a growing ability to determine an author's purpose and point of view, and use this information as a springboard for thinking and conversations with a critical edge
- Evidence of a growing awareness of the qualities that define a hero, the role of heroes in our nation and the world, and our own ability to act heroically

DETERMINE EVIDENCE OF DEVELOPING ABILITIES

Talk offers keen insight into a child's thinking. When we listen intently as children use talk to build and verify theories, we get a glimpse of their strategy use in action, their capacity and propensity to think with others purposefully, and their ability to use a range of resources thoughtfully.

So powerful is talk as an indicator of thinking and as a tool for strengthening thinking that the unit design features sample bits of talk we would hope to hear. This includes talk that's indicative of children's growing ability with multiple sources of information and talk that's indicative of their growing understanding of the concept of a hero.

It's important to note that the possible talk indicators are written in language that may seem sophisticated for third grade. What we have learned in all of our teaching, however, is that the more sophisticated the language we use with children, the more sophisticated the language they will produce. We aim high, model to meet these lofty goals, and realize that, in reality, we will hear these ideas expressed in a range of language forms that represent the developmental range of our children.

Oral language is not the only mode of communication available as assessment. At certain points in the unit, we might collect written evidence of the children's thinking by having them jot down ideas or things they notice in an ongoing response journal. As much as we consistently strive to collect ongoing anecdotal evidence as we confer with our children or join in on their conversations, having children commit their thinking to writing offers added insights.

Units may also be designed to culminate in a project that represents understanding. To be representative of the depth of understanding, these projects should move beyond reporting to persuasive efforts or other means that highlight children actually using the knowledge they have constructed. Chapter 8 illustrates a few possibilities.

Determine Instructional Focus Points Within the Unit

Once the goals for the unit of study are decided, along with strong foundational understandings about the nature of the teaching and learning inside the unit, it's time to plan the actual flow of instruction. This process most often begins by considering a progression of instructional focus points that need to be emphasized throughout the unit.

In this particular unit, instruction focused on the process of reading, thinking, and talking among multiple sources of information would be a key element. Although the children had some experience with multiple sources under their belt, it certainly was not sufficient. Jeralyn and I knew that her children would need support with selecting text sets, planning a progression through the text set, understanding each source on its own, and thinking between two sources and then among multiple sources. The unit overview (Figure 6.1, pp. 86–88) highlights this emphasis in the "What to teach" column. The "Why" column reminds us to maintain a focus on critical understandings of sources and ideas.

As we consider the social studies standards integrated into this unit, it's clear that the children will not fully realize the breadth and depth suggested by those standards in this unit. However, they will build a strong base of content knowledge that will elevate the level of further social studies instruction.

SELECTING SOURCES OF INFORMATION

The next step in unit design is to select the sources of information for whole-group instruction. These sources may be used for read-alouds, shared reading, or in specific mini-lessons. As suggested in Chapter 4, children need to be taught the importance of careful consideration of the progression through sources in a text set. Beginning with sources that offer easy access to foundational information necessary to begin the process of understanding is often crucial for success. Decisions about what genres, text types, and media forms are needed to expand comprehension and ways to locate these sources become teaching points in our unit design.

Text sets used instructionally should vary in the number and variety of sources of information so children don't infer that a specified number of sources or range of sources is always necessary or adequate. Text sets should remain flexible, giving children the option of swapping sources, adding on, or not progressing through all sources if they feel it's not necessary.

In "What Is an American Hero?" only the first person to be studied and the first text set were pre-selected. The children joined in on the decision-making about other individuals to be studied and about the number and range of sources that would build a strong text set. Because of this decision to release responsibility for the decision-making process, our unit overview and day-to-day planning were designed with some vagueness. The sources used, however, have been added to the overview and day-by-day lesson design (Figure 6.2) for the purpose of illustrating the unit as completely as possible.

PLANNING THE PROGRESSION OF LESSONS AND THE RESULTING PARTNERSHIP AND INDEPENDENT WORK

Once the unit overview is completed, we begin to plan for a flow of instruction throughout the unit. This day-by-day envisioning of our teaching, as laid out in Figure 6.2 (see pp. 92–96), is the most dynamic portion of the planning. We anticipate the way we think the work will progress based on what we know about our children and our goals, knowing full well that there will be wobbles along the way. A source may take longer to read, think, and talk about than we had planned, for a variety of reasons. It may be more challenging than we anticipated, or the children may dig deeper into it than we had thought. Or, the class might become so enamored with or puzzled by one of our subjects that we take on an additional source of information to support them in sorting things out. We may find that our partnerships need a pause to reflect on purposeful talk behavior, or that we need to dig deeper into particular comprehension strategies.

Even knowing there will be adjustments along the way, we plan out the workshop lessons and corresponding partnership and independent explorations for the same reason we do our yearlong planning and our unit planning—we need to hold onto a sense of where we are going. In this way, we are able to adjust thoughtfully, considering the implications on our children's progression through the whole of the study and the yearlong curriculum design.

What clearly seems to be missing from the day-to-day design are mini-lessons. Mini-lessons, as discussed in Chapter 5, are quick lessons designed to remind children of comprehension work, talk behavior, organizational strategies, or other issues that pop up along the way. As mini-lessons are very responsive to children's needs, they are often designed a day or two prior to instruction. For this reason, the content of the mini-lessons was not part of our unit planning.

You may have noted that this unit lays out only whole-group and partnership and independent work. We know that small-group instruction that meets very specific needs of our children is crucial for success. Our small-group instruction is planned not just with this work in mind, but with a wide range of needs our students may have as possible focus points.

Figure 6.2: WHAT IS AN AMERICAN HERO? WEEK 1					
Whole-class instruction	Teacher models the selection of a text set through a think-aloud, thoughtfully choosing a few texts from a larger set of texts about the person the class will study together.	The teacher chooses which source to read first from the text set, thinking aloud and explaining the rationale for reading this text first. Read aloud *George Washington* by Lola Schafer with purposeful talk designed to build strong understanding with a critical edge. Revisit portion of the source for a comprehension mini-lesson. Begin charting qualities of George Washington.	The teacher chooses which text from the text set will be second in the progression, giving the rationale. Read aloud *George Washington, First President* by Mike Venezia, with purposeful talk designed to build strong understanding with a critical edge. Revisit portion of the source for a comprehension mini-lesson. Continue charting qualities of George Washington.	The teacher uses a mix of rereading and shared reading to support the children in comparing and contrasting the information the first two authors presented on the person being studied. Children begin to make decisions about whether George Washington is an American hero, and why. The class begins a chart defining an American hero.	The teacher chooses which source to read third, thinking aloud and explaining the rationale. Read aloud (view) the Mt. Vernon Web site with purposeful talk designed to build strong understanding with a critical edge. Revisit portion of the source for a comprehension mini-lesson. Continue charting qualities of George Washington. Add to definition of an American hero if the opportunity presents itself.
Partner and independent work	Children explore possible sources for this study, considering candidates for the designation of hero.	Children continue to browse through choices for their study of heroes. They begin to consider who they would like to study, and browse through sources that will help them to decide.	Children select the person they will study, and partnerships are formed based on selection. (Teacher support is needed to guide the formation of strong, successful partnerships.) Partners work on the thoughtful selection of a text set. When possible, they collect double copies so they are able to read the same source at the same time.	Partners plan their progression through the text set, and rethink any text set choices that may not quite work out. They discuss their launch source and get started.	Children prepare for independent reading with a partner planning meeting, read independently, then meet in partnerships to discuss and construct deeper meaning. They may choose to chart as was done in the whole-group study.

Expanding Comprehension With Multigenre Text Sets

Figure 6.2: WHAT IS AN AMERICAN HERO? WEEK 2					
Whole-class instruction	Teacher uses a mix of rereading and shared reading to support the children in thinking among the big ideas the first two authors presented and the big ideas from the third source. Thoughts about George Washington's qualities are added to the chart. Thoughts about the definition of a hero are added to the hero chart if the opportunity presents itself.	Teacher chooses which source to read as the fourth from the text set, thinking aloud and explaining the rationale. Read aloud *Stories for Young Patriots* by Lynne Cheney, with purposeful talk designed to build strong understanding with a critical edge. Revisit portion of the source for a comprehension mini-lesson.	Teacher uses a mix of rereading and shared reading to support the children in thinking among the prior three sources and the big ideas from the fourth source. Thoughts about George Washington's qualities are added to the chart. Thoughts about the definition of a hero are added to the hero chart if the opportunity presents itself.	Teacher chooses which source to read fifth from the text set, thinking aloud and explaining the rationale. Read aloud the first half of *George Washington* by Cheryl Harness (this is a dense text) with purposeful talk designed to build strong understanding with a critical edge. Encourage the children to think and talk among all sources.Note: If children seem to need a day to think among sources before a new source is added, slow the process down and do so. Revisit portion of the source for a comprehension mini-lesson.	Read aloud the second half of *George Washington* by Cheryl Harness, with purposeful talk designed to build strong understanding with a critical edge. Encourage the children to think and talk among all sources. Revisit portion of the source for a comprehension mini-lesson.
Partner and independent work	Children prepare for independent reading with a partner planning meeting, read independently, then meet in partnerships to discuss and construct deeper meaning. As partners move into their second source, they begin to think and talk between sources, and ask questions.	Children prepare for independent reading with a partner planning meeting, read independently, then meet in partnerships to discuss and construct deeper meaning. As partners move into their third source, they begin to think and talk among sources, and continue to ask questions. Note: Not all partnerships will be into their third source at this point.	Children prepare for independent reading with a partner planning meeting, read independently, then meet in partnerships to discuss and construct deeper meaning.	Children prepare for independent reading with a partner planning meeting, read independently, then meet in partnerships to discuss and construct deeper meaning. They continue to think among sources, ask questions, and possibly chart. Some may need to exchange sources in their text sets.	Children prepare for independent reading with a partner planning meeting, read independently, then meet in partnerships to discuss and construct deeper meaning.

Figure 6.2: WHAT IS AN AMERICAN HERO? WEEK 3

Whole-class instruction				
Teacher chooses which source to read sixth from the text set, thinking aloud and explaining the rationale.	The class decides on a new individual to study. They use a shared process to select a text set from a larger collection of texts, and make decisions about the progression through the text set.	Read aloud *Ben Franklin: Man of Many Talents* by Time for Kids with purposeful talk designed to build strong understanding with a critical edge. Encourage the children to think and talk between both sources.	Read aloud (view) *The Ben Show* (video clip), with purposeful talk designed to build strong understanding with a critical edge. Encourage the children to think and talk among all three sources.	Read aloud (view) *Benjamin Franklin: Scientist and Inventor* (Animated Hero Classic), with purposeful talk designed to build strong understanding with a critical edge. Encourage the children to think and talk among all sources.
Read aloud *George Washington's Teeth* by Deborah Chandra and Madeleine Comora, with purposeful talk designed to build strong understanding with a critical edge. Encourage the children to think and talk among all sources.	Read aloud *Benjamin Franklin* by Philip Abraham with purposeful talk designed to build strong understanding with a critical edge.	Revisit portion of the source for a comprehension mini-lesson.	Revisit portion of the source for a comprehension mini-lesson. Note: If children seem to need a day to think among sources before a new source is added, slow the process down and do so.	Note: As we knew children would need one viewing to just enjoy this film, we had them watch it outside the workshop. This was a second viewing focused on understanding Ben and thinking critically about the source.
Revisit portion of the source for a comprehension mini-lesson.	Revisit portion of the source for a comprehension mini-lesson.	Add to the Benjamin Franklin chart, the progression through a text set chart, and the definition of a hero chart.	Add to the qualities chart, the progression through a text set chart, and the definition of a hero chart.	Revisit portion of the source for a comprehension mini-lesson.
Children and teacher reflect on their work through three lenses: • Big ideas about George Washington • Thinking about what qualities define an American hero, and how this knowledge helps us to shape our lives • Reflection on the process of reading, thinking, and talking among sources, and how it might help us in our everyday lives.	Begin a chart of the qualities of Benjamin Franklin. A new chart is started to track the progression through a text set.			Add to the qualities chart, the progression through a text set chart, and the definition of a hero chart.

Partner and independent work				
Children prepare for independent reading with a partner planning meeting, read independently, then meet in partnerships to discuss and construct deeper meaning.	Children prepare for independent reading with a partner planning meeting, read independently, then meet in partnerships to sum up their thinking about the person they have been studying.	Children discuss any lingering thoughts about the person they have been studying, and revisit sources to clarify or strengthen ideas.	Children wrap up their study by spreading out the texts they have read, discussing what they learned, which sources were most powerful and why, and the progression of their thinking.	Partners choose a new person to study, and select sources for their text set. They plan their progression through the text set, and begin with their launch source if time allows. The progression through a text set chart, created during whole class instruction, supports this process (see Figure 4.2, p. 54).

Expanding Comprehension With Multigenre Text Sets

Whole-class instruction	Read aloud *How Benjamin Stole the Lightning* by Rosalyn Schanzer, with purposeful talk designed to build strong understanding with a critical edge. Encourage the children to think and talk among all sources. Revisit portion of the source for a comprehension mini-lesson. Children and teacher reflect on their work through three lenses: • Big ideas about Benjamin Franklin. • Thinking about what qualities define an American her, and how this knowledge helps us to shape our lives. • Reflection on the process of reading, thinking, and talking among sources, and how it might help us in our everyday lives.	The class decides on a new individual to study. They use a shared process to select a text set from a larger collection of texts, and make decisions about the progression through the text set. Read aloud *Amelia Earhart* by Wil Mara, with purposeful talk designed to build strong understanding with a critical edge. Revisit portion of the source for a comprehension mini-lesson. Begin a chart of the qualities of Amelia Earhart. Add to the definition of a heo chart if the opportunity presents itself.	Read aloud *Amelia Earhart* by Marilyn Rosenthal and Daniel Freeman, with purposeful talk designed to build strong understanding with a critical edge. Encourage the children to think and talk between both sources. Note: If children seem to need a day to think among sources before a new source is added, slow down the process and do so. Revisit portion of the source for a comprehension mini-lesson. Add to the qualities chart and the definition of a hero chart. Begin expanded text chart discussed in Chapter 5 (figure 5.1, p. 76).	Read aloud page 4 of *Amelia to Zora: Twenty-Six Women Who Changed the World* by Cynthia Chin-Lee and viewing of an Amelia clip on YouTube, with purposeful talk designed to build strong understanding with a critical edge. Encourage the children to think and talk among all sources. Note: The two sources were brief, so we decided to take on both. Revisit portion of the source for a comprehension mini-lesson. Add to the qualities chart, the definition of a hero chart, and the text set chart..	Read aloud "Miss Earhart Forced Down at Sea, Howland Isle Fears; Coast Guard Begins Search" from the *New York Times Magazine*, with purposeful talk designed to build strong understanding with a critical edge. Encourage the children to think and talk among all sources. Revisit portion of the source for a comprehension mini-lesson. Add to the qualities chart, the definition of a hero chart, and the text set chart.
Partner and independent work	Children prepare for independent reading with a partner planning meeting, read independently, then meet in partnerships to discuss and construct deeper meaning. Some partnerships may choose to chart their thinking.	Children prepare for independent reading with a partner planning meeting, read independently, then meet in partnerships to discuss and construct deeper meaning. Partners push each other to think and talk among sources, and ask questions to propel their learning.	Children prepare for independent reading with a partner planning meeting, read independently, then meet in partnerships to discuss and construct deeper meaning.	Children prepare for independent reading with a partner planning meeting, read independently, then meet in partnerships to discuss and construct deeper meaning.	Children prepare for independent reading with a partner planning meeting, read independently, then meet in partnerships to discuss and construct deeper meaning.

Figure 6.2: WHAT IS AN AMERICAN HERO? WEEK 4

Whole class instruction	Read aloud *Amelia and Eleanor Go For a Ride* by Pam Muñoz Ryan, with purposeful talk designed to build strong understanding with a critical edge. Revisit portion of the source for a comprehension mini-lesson. Add to the qualities chart, the definition of a hero chart, and the text set chart. Children and teacher reflect on their work through three lenses: • Big ideas about Amelia Earhart • Thinking about what qualities define an American hero, and how this knowledge helps us to shape our lives • Reflection on the process of reading, thinking, and talking among sources, and how it might help us in our everyday lives.	The class decides on a new individual to study. They use a shared process to select a text set from a larger collection of texts, and make decisions about the progression through the text set. Read aloud *I've Seen the Promised Land: The Life of Dr. Martin Luther King, Jr.,* by Walter Dean Myers, with purposeful talk designed to build strong understanding with a critical edge. Revisit portion of the source for a comprehension mini-lesson. Begin a chart of the qualities of Dr. Martin Luther King, Jr. Add to the definition of a hero chart if the opportunity presents itself.	Read aloud *Life in the Times of Rosa Parks and the Civil Rights Movement* by Terri Degezelle (Heinemann Library), with purposeful talk designed to build strong understanding with a critical edge. Encourage the children to think and talk between both sources. Revisit portion of the source for a comprehension mini-lesson. Add to the qualities chart and the definition of a hero chart.	Read aloud *Freedom Summer* by Deborah Wiles, with purposeful talk designed to build strong understanding with a critical edge. Encourage the children to think and talk among all sources. Revisit portion of one of the source for a comprehension mini-lesson. Add to the qualities chart and the definition of a hero chart.	Read aloud of a portion of the "I Have A Dream" speech and view a portion of a video clip of Dr. King delivering the speech, with purposeful talk designed to build strong understanding with a critical edge. Encourage the children to think and talk among all sources. Revisit portion of the source for a comprehension mini-lesson. Add to the qualities chart and the definition of a hero chart. Children and teacher reflect on their work through three lenses: • Big ideas about Amelia Earhart • Thinking about what qualities define an American hero, and how this knowledge helps us to shape our lives • Reflection on the process of reading, thinking, and talking among sources, and how it might help us in our everyday lives.
Partner and independent work	Children prepare for independent reading with a partner planning meeting, read independently, then meet in partnerships to discuss and construct deeper meaning.	Children prepare for independent reading with a partner planning meeting, read independently, and then meet in partnerships to sum up their thinking about the person they have been studying.	Children discuss any lingering thoughts about the person they have been studying, and revisit sources to clarify or strengthen ideas.	Children wrap up their study by spreading out the texts they have read, discussing what they learned, which sources were most powerful and why, and how their thinking progressed.	Children swap partners and share their thinking about the heroes they discovered and the process of reading, thinking, and talking among sources of information.

Although this unit lays out only our reading work, our literacy instruction is not complete without turning our attention to writing as one means of sharing our thinking with the world. As children read, think, and talk among texts, they are forming thoughts and opinions about what constitutes a hero, who can truly be considered a hero, and what roles heroes play in shaping our world. This thinking can and should be communicated to others. In this way, this unit plan for the reading workshop would lie nicely next to a writing workshop unit that draws on this knowledge to craft a range of texts, including reports, feature articles, or persuasive essays. The work might also fuel opportunities to create texts in other media forms including video, PowerPoint, or mixed media pieces. Again, Chapter 8 will explore some of these possibilities.

This unit of study design, both the overview and the day-to-day planning, reflects a suggested progression for children who are in a particular place in their abilities with reading, thinking, and talking among multiple sources, and with comprehension strategies. As you consider your children and wonder whether this unit will serve them as is, there are questions you need to consider. Will my children need more work with reading between two texts before moving into multiple sources? Are there specific ways of thinking and talking about reading (comprehension strategies) I need to build into these lessons? Are our partnerships effective? Is the children's ability with purposeful talk strong?

Then, of course, there is the work and process of locating sources of information to be considered. Are the sources suggested appropriate for my children? If I need to substitute sources, what sources of information do I have access to? Will some of the texts I use for whole-group instruction need more than the days allotted? Thinking through these and other questions that occur will allow you to redesign this unit to meet the unique needs of your children—a crucial step in any curriculum planning.

Chapter 7

Understanding Big Ideas in Our World

> It is not once nor twice but times without number that
> the same ideas make their appearance in the world.
> ~Aristotle

ERIC: Yeah—they're all jealous—

DARRELL: Yeah—because jealousy—it's a big idea and a lot of stuff makes you feel it. 'Cause she
(holding up *Julius, the Baby of the World*) had a baby brother, and lots of kids are jealous of that.
And this other one (pointing to *Peter's Chair*)—he had a baby, too, who was getting all his stuff.

ERIC: But this one (pointing to *Memory String*) doesn't have a baby. It's a new—new— like a mom.
She's jealous of that, 'cause her dad pays the mom lots of attention. So she's jealous of something different. Not a baby.

Units of study that teach children to read, think, and talk among multiple sources of information,
and continue to strengthen these abilities, should be designed for children across grade levels
and incorporate a range of inquiry possibilities. The snippet of conversation above came from
a second-grade partnership explaining the text set they were creating to explore the big idea of jealousy.
The two boys were sorting through texts the class had already read, thought about, and talked about
together, and put into a book tub labeled "Jealousy." The boys had chosen *Julius, the Baby of the World* by
Kevin Henkes, *Peter's Chair* by Ezra Jack Keats, and *The Memory String* by Eve Bunting. Although the
text set to this point comprised only picture books, the choices were powerful, and the boys had a strong
sense of how each fit.

While the "What Is an American Hero?" inquiry was supported predominately by nonfiction sources of information, this isn't the case with all studies. As children explore realistic fiction in depth, they
develop the realization that the authors of these texts are calling on the reader to ponder big ideas about
the world. Rather than containing children's thinking and talking within single texts, we can just as eas-

ily expand children's exploration of these ideas by designing studies that encourage them to explore the ideas across a range of sources. By doing this, we ensure that children are reading to understand *ideas* as opposed to understanding *texts*. Again, as with our hero unit, our push is toward helping children to use this understanding of ideas to shape the way they live in the world. As with our predominantly non-fiction studies, we create text sets for studies of big ideas that draw upon a range of genres, text types, and media forms, including picture books, chapter books or novels, poetry, historical fiction, biography, photographs, Web sites, and video.

Whereas our hero sources were most often grouped into book tubs by topics to support the construction of text sets, studies of big ideas require sources to be grouped by these ideas. This necessitates some understanding of the big ideas inside a range of sources prior to the creation of the text sets.

The deeper the understanding the children construct of fiction sources during the first read or subsequent revisits, the better able they are to group these sources together into text sets based on big ideas. This deep understanding of fiction sources is predicated on children's ability to construct a strong understanding of characters, setting, and events, and the way the interplay among these elements causes change. This work generally begins in kindergarten, with children identifying characters and settings, and progresses across grades to an understanding of big ideas and beyond as children identify archetypal characters and story lines, search for symbolism, and critically question authors' perceptions of the world.

The following study of big ideas in the world was designed for a fifth-grade class following a study of theme, or big ideas, in single sources. The children had some experience reading, thinking, and talking among multiple sources, but had returned to single sources to build a library of known realistic fiction texts to enable them to construct text sets based on big ideas. When their teacher, Elaina, and I designed the study, shown in Figure 7.1 (see pp. 101–103), we began with the following essential questions:

- What big ideas about the world do these authors want us to think about?
- How do different authors convey thoughts about these big ideas?
- How can I use my understanding to live thoughtfully in the world?
- How does reading, thinking, and talking among multiple sources of information help us understand?

Expanding Comprehension With Multigenre Text Sets

Figure 7.1: READING UNIT OF INQUIRY
HOW DO AUTHORS HELP US TO UNDERSTAND BIG IDEAS? GRADE 5

Essential questions	• What big ideas about the world do these authors want us to think about? • How do different authors convey thoughts about these big ideas? • How can I use my understanding to live thoughtfully in the world? • How do reading, thinking, and talking among multiple sources of information help us to understand?				
Desired results	• Evidence of ongoing strengthening of the children's ability to read, think, and talk among sources of information in a range of text types, genres, and media forms • Evidence of an ability to determine an author's purpose and point of view, and use this information as a springboard for thinking and conversations with a critical edge • Evidence of ability to use understandings from this process to act thoughtfully in the world				

What to teach	**Why**	**Instructional approach**	**Sources of information**	**What might talk indicative of strong comprehension sound like?**	**What might talk indicative of strong reading, thinking, and talking among sources sound like?**
Creating text sets	Children need support in selecting a range of sources on a topic, and understanding how this range of sources expands comprehension.	Model the selection of texts, and think aloud about thoughtful progression through texts.	**Perseverance:** • *The Lemonade Club* by Patricia Polacco • *The Harmonica* by Tony Johnston and Ron Mazellan • *Baseball Saved Us* by Ken Mochizuki • *Jump! From the Life of Michael Jordan* by Floyd Cooper • "Amazing Aquatics: Hundreds of New Animal Species Discovered Off the Coast of Australia" by Lara Anderson http://www2. scholastic.com/ browse/article • "Perseverance" Derek Redmond http://www. youtube.com/ tch?v=Nifq3 Ke2Q3o **The importance of family:** • *My Rotten Redheaded Older Brother* by Patricia Polacco • *Our Gracie Aunt* by Jacqueline Woodson *continued*		• I want to think more about __, so I'll need books that are . . . • I better start with a basic/easy book because I don't know much about . . . • I know __ (author) writes about this big idea. Let me see how he/she addresses this issue. • The sources I've read are all fiction. I wonder if I can find a nonfiction source that addresses this issue. • I have all traditional texts. I wonder what I'll find online, or if any videos have explored this big idea . . .

Figure 7.1: READING UNIT OF INQUIRY
HOW DO AUTHORS HELP US TO UNDERSTAND BIG IDEAS? GRADE 5

Under-standing each source deeply on its own	Children need to think and talk about each source, pushing to-wards critical understand-ings. Readers then need to integrate this information with their own beliefs and un-derstandings to strengthen or challenge them, and con-tinue to ask questions.	Combine read-aloud and shared reading with purpose-ful talk to build strong com-prehension of each text and study the strategy used as readers to construct strong mean-ing.	• *Aunt Flossie's Hats (and Crab Cakes Later)* 10th Anniversary Edition with Author's Afterword and Family Photographs by Elizabeth Fitzgerald Howard • Disney Family http://family.go.com/ • Barack Obama's Family Photo Album http://www.youtube.com/watch?v=opjDZPp-JQc • "The Accident" from *Baseball, Snakes and Summer Squash* by Donald Graves • "Teamwork" from *Relatively Speaking* by Ralph Fletcher	• This character makes me think . . . • This character's behavior caused . . . • The events in this story are caused by . . . • This way the author crafted the characters and the change in the story has me thinking . . . • This author really wants me to think about . . . • The author's point of view seems to be . . . • This author's ideas make me think . . . • Before I read this, I thought . . . • Now I'm more sure of . . . • Now, I'm wondering . . . • I feel the same way when . . . • I notice this same thing happening in the real world when . . .	• The authors of all of these sources have the same point of view. I wonder if I can find an author who has a differ-ent point of view. • I'm noticing that the texts I'm finding are all (biography, informa-tional, traditional texts, etc.). I wonder if I can find a different (genre, text type, media form) to help with my thinking. • It's interesting the way some authors of fiction write about the same big ideas as authors of nonfiction. They are really writing about the world through made-up characters and events. I think they do this be-cause all these sources together help me to . . .
Reading, thinking, and talking among texts	Once a single source is understood, it needs to be held up to other sources. Children need to engage in thinking and talking with a critical edge. Do the facts match? Are the author's big ideas the same? Why or why not? Do the authors have the same purpose and point of view?	Modeled and shared reading with purpose-ful talk	**Understanding people who are different from us:** • *The Summer My Father Was Ten* by Pat Brisson • *Me and Mr. Mah* by Andrea Spalding and Janet Wilson • *Chicken Sunday* by Patricia Polacco • *Seedfolks* by Paul Fleischman • "Disabilities Don't Hold These Olympians Back" from *Scholastic News*, Kid Reporter Allie Sakowicz http://news.scholastic.com/scholastic_news_online/2008/04/disabilities-do.html *continued*	• At his point, all of my reading, thinking, and conversations with others has me thing. . . • I think I will read/reread __ (title of source) because now I'm wondering . . . • I'm not noticing that the characters in all of these sources are affected by . . .	

Figure 7.1: READING UNIT OF INQUIRY
HOW DO AUTHORS HELP US TO UNDERSTAND BIG IDEAS? GRADE 5

Continually constructing a stronger understanding, and developing my own point of view	As readers think and talk about a range of sources, they continuously construct and shape stronger critical understandings. Little by little the readers begin to form their own point of view.	Modeled and shared reading with purposeful talk	**Feeling Proud:** • *The Unbreakable Code* by Sara Hoagland Hunter • *Owl Moon* by Jane Yolen • *The Wednesday Surprise* by Eve Bunting • *Strong to the Hoop* by John Coy • *Rosa* by Nikki Giovanni • The Story on Self Esteem http://kidshealth.org/kid/feeling/emotion/self_esteem.html • Spain Reigns http://www2.scholastic.com/browse/article.jsp?id=3749788	• Now that I've read many sources and talked with others, I'm beginning to think . . . • At first I thought . . . I still think . . . or Now I'm beginning to change my thinking because . . .	
Using this information to live smartly in the world	Knowledge is power if we use it in thoughtful ways. Children often need support in using what they know to generate new knowledge and shape their world.	Thinking and talking together, and modeling ways of using knowledge		• Now that I know __, I think I should . . . (action) • I want to tell _ to try to get him/her thinking about . . . • Others should be interested in this because . . .	• Reading, thinking and talking among all of these sources really helped me because . . . • I've been wondering about . . . Now I know I need to read more sources and think and talk with more people to figure it out.

Elaina and I wanted to get a head start on the construction of the first text set, but we also wanted the children to join in on the decisions based on their understandings of the texts they had been reading, thinking, and talking about in their theme unit. We decided to begin with *The Harmonica* by Tony Johnston and *The Lemonade Club* by Patricia Polacco. These two texts have very different literal topics, but both touch on the big idea of perseverance. Our hope was that, by thinking and talking between these two texts, children would develop an awareness of the ways each author touched on this big idea, and be able to suggest other texts that did the same. Let's listen in as Elaina gets the children started.

ELAINA: (holding up a copy of *The Harmonica* by Tony Johnston) The author of this text had very
    important thoughts about the world—

FELIPE: Yeah—that one was really powerful.

ELAINA: Powerful how?

FELIPE: It made us think how you have to be clever and not give up.

ELAINA: Patricia Polacco got us thinking about the idea of not giving up in *The Lemonade Club*, too. How did Patricia do this?

CHELSEA: It was about something different—not war, but the character had to not give up, because she was sick. She had to keep trying to be strong.

ELAINA: Did any of the other texts we read get us thing about not giving up?

MIKE: Well, yeah, because other characters had hard times—like the character in that one (pointing to *Baseball Saved Us* by Ken Mochizuki over in the library).

TRINA: Well, yeah, because they both had war, and the characters, they both had to be smart to figure it out.

KEISHA: If they gave up, they wouldn't survive.

ELAINA: There's a word for that. It's called *perseverance*. Perseverance is when we try and try, and keep going even when it's hard.

MIKE: Oh, yeah—we said that when we read (pointing to the library, runs over to the folk literature tub, rifles through, and pulls out a book of Aesop's fables) this book.

ELAINA: Oh— "The Tortoise and the Hare"?

CHILDREN: Oh, yeah!

ELAINA: So we have three authors who wrote about perseverance in different ways. Why?

JACQUELINE: Well, it's like for thinking—they want—the authors want us to know about the world and the important ideas. They write about them so we think more about them.

ELAINA: Do you think other authors write about perseverance?

FRANCISCO: Well—probably.

Elaina: Let's do this. Let's take time to explore books we've already read and know well. Work with your partner and rethink the author's big ideas. Let's see if we can gather books we think have messages about perseverance—we'll make a text set, so we're able to think more about this big idea.

The children head off to the classroom library with their partners. Some partners rush in, grab a specific book, and immediately begin flipping pages and talking. Other partnerships hover at the edge of the library area, scanning shelves, a little unsure. Elaina and I began moving among the partnerships, supporting those who are unsure, and encouraging the thinking of those who are on to something.

When the children regroup at the carpet, they have a range of texts, including a few biographies and nonfiction sources from previous studies. After much deliberation, we ended up with a text set for whole-group study.

Our instruction inside this text set, bolstered by a few sources we slipped in to add breadth, followed a similar flow as outlined in the first-week description of "What Is an American Hero?" The flow

Expanding Comprehension With Multigenre Text Sets

was similar simply because these fifth graders were at the same point in their understanding of drawing from multiple sources as our third-grade children.

As with our "What Is an American Hero?" study, the children prepared for partner and independent reading by creating their own text sets. Partners decided on big ideas to explore, and chose texts from a mix of picture books, poems, chapter books, biographies, and some photos that had been placed in the big idea book tubs. Additionally, the children played a role in creating the next text sets for whole-group study. These text sets, which ended up exploring pride, the importance of family, and understanding people who are different from us, are also listed in the unit overview. As with the perseverance text set, Elaina and I added sources to expand the range of genres, text types, and media forms when possible. We did the same with the text sets children formed for their partner and independent reading.

The toughest part of creating text sets around big ideas was that there were so many possibilities, so many passionately crafted texts that spoke to the big ideas we were studying. Paring the text sets down to a manageable size became a matter of negotiating choices. We still ended up with too many sources, and balanced between completely rereading some and revisiting parts of others so we could think and talk through an author's perspective on the big idea under study, as well as ways of crafting a story around that big idea.

What's of crucial importance in this unit, as with all units, is that the conversations resulting from pursuing big ideas across multiple sources help the children consider their own interactions with others, using what they know to shape their world.

The following conversational snippet illustrates this well.

KENESHIA: So it's like everybody's life is different, but we all have troubles. Having perseverance helps us get through.

JARED: Not just hard times. Like Michael Jordan didn't have it so hard. He just wanted something really bad.

MITCHELL: Yeah—what they're all saying [the authors] is if you give up, you definitely won't make it. But if you have perseverance, you have hope.

JARED: It's like us with our lives. If we really want something or yeah, if it's hard, we—we have to have perseverance.

The children's expanded understanding of big ideas (in this case, perseverance), was enabling them to envision living in the world thoughtfully.

Chapter 8

Sharing Our Growing Understanding With Others

〜〜〜〜〜〜〜〜

> If you would not be forgotten as soon as you are dead,
> either write things worth reading, or do things worth writing.
> ~ Benjamin Franklin

One of my favorite weekend pursuits, a throwback to days prior to one-click access to any news source imaginable, is curling up with coffee and the Sunday newspaper. The part of the paper I savor most, and always save for last, is the op-ed section. In our San Diego paper, this section is called "Dialogue," a title that speaks to my heart. After all the columns and letters, the best part is to be found on the last page—the editor's picks for the best political cartoons from around the country that week. I revel in these cartoons and their creators, whether I agree with them or not. In them, I see a marriage of knowledge and imagination, a knowledge of world events that reveals a depth of understanding, and an imagination that allows the cartoonist to share his or her point of view in a way that informs, entertains, and attempts to persuade, all rolled into one.

From Ben Franklin's "Join or Die" to those old episodes of *Rocky and Bullwinkle*, oozing with political commentary, and today's *South Park*, cartoons in a variety of media have spanned the ages as a way of sharing thinking. And that's just for starters. Authors draw from a wide range of genres, text types, and media forms to interject their thinking into our lives. Formal and informal, persuasive, entertaining, informative or not, well-thought-through or off-the-cuff—the need to share our thinking with others is part of who we are as humans.

When we've invested time in thinking deeply about an issue or idea, and have formed our own point of view, the urge to put our thoughts out into the world often intensifies. We share for a variety of interconnected reasons. We may hope to inform, offering our best theory to support others as they embark on the same intellectual journey. We may use our knowledge to entertain or, if we feel passionate about the idea or issue, we may attempt to craft our thoughts in a persuasive manner. These endeavors may be casual—talking, e-mailing, or debating with friends. Or, we may enter into more formal arenas by speaking out at a public hearing, creating a PowerPoint presentation or video, writing letters to the editor, or starting a Web site.

Knowing that actions speak directly to our beliefs, many prefer to allow their deeds to convey their thoughts. Understanding, for instance, the qualities of a hero and the impact heroes have on our world should change our behavior. As Maya Angelou said, "When people show you who they are, believe them." Beyond revealing a sense of self, when children understand that their constructed understandings can shape their actions, and these actions have the potential to shape their world, they are transforming into informed, participating members of society.

While contexts for sharing our thinking and methods of sharing our thinking differ, the act of sharing is always driven by purpose. Sharing our thinking isn't about good grades or external approval. We don't share our newly constructed political wisecrack in hopes of getting an A in the oral wisecrack genre. We genuinely want to make a point while sharing a laugh with friends. We don't write a letter to the editor hoping to ace grammar and punctuation. Rather, we hope to right a perceived wrong or bring attention to something we deem worthy. We share our thinking with the intent of having an impact on others.

When children put Herculean effort into understanding complex ideas and issues, involving them in opportunities to share their thinking with others allows them to use their knowledge purposefully and feel its power. This also allows us an additional opportunity to determine growth and next steps and to assess the effectiveness of our instruction.

In assessing the projects and products that result from these opportunities, we look for evidence of a range of developing abilities based on our unit goals. Questions such as the following (one of which is specific to the "What Is an American Hero?" unit) help us observe children engaged in the process of creating projects and products and the end result of that process.

- Does the author draw from a range of sources of information, with a mix of genres, text types, and media forms, to form his or her own opinion?
- Does the author have a thoughtful point of view, with evidence to support his or her thinking?
- Does the author transition from a topic to ideas or issues inside the topic (movement from literal understanding to deeper comprehension)?
- Does the author offer a compilation of information, or a synthesis?
- Does the author have a strong sense of purpose?
- Does the author understand the concept of hero and the effect heroes have in our world?

Expanding Comprehension With Multigenre Text Sets

Other assessment tools, such as writing rubrics, may support us in observing both the process and end result of children's efforts to share their thinking. Again, what is crucial is that these projects or products be conceived as opportunities to learn more about our children, rethink our curricular design, and allow children to connect knowledge and action in a way that transforms their sense of themselves in the world—not as an act of assign-and-grade.

Let's explore just a few of the possibilities for sharing the depth and breadth of ideas constructed by reading, thinking, and talking among multiple sources of information. These suggestions are focused on providing authentic opportunities for children to share their thinking with the world for the purpose of affecting others while offering teachers an opportunity to assess both the process and end product of their efforts.

Sharing Our Thinking Through Our Actions

Several days after Manuel, Alani, and Toya hung a sign reminding their classmates of the link between behavior and reputation on the classroom door (Figure 2.4, p. 30), a new, larger sign appeared. This sign read, "Think before you walk through this door. Act like a hero." This sign, it seemed, was the end result of a conversation about the qualities of a hero and the reasons these qualities mattered long ago and still matter today.

Through this conversation, the children came to the realization that many of these qualities were ways of living in the world heroically that they could strive toward. They vowed to use this understanding, as well as the class's understanding of the importance of reputation, to shape their actions, and through their actions try to effect change in others. The sign, made by two of the children, was a reminder each time they left the classroom and headed out into the world. This linking of knowledge to actions is a crucial step in helping children feel the impact of their efforts, and it is an honest, powerful way to share beliefs with others.

Sharing Our Thinking as an Oral Product

Talking with others is essential to constructing a broad understanding of complex issues and ideas. We talk purposefully as a means of immersing ourselves in a range of perspectives and navigating our way through confusions. Once our thoughts are formed, we continue talking with others, but we weave in and out of different types of talk. We keep talking purposefully to expand meaning, knowing full well that new thinking will continue to evolve our understanding of complex issues and ideas. But we also begin to talk to share the meaning we have constructed—our own well-thought-through point of view.

ORAL PRESENTATIONS AND SPEECHES

This sharing of thinking may be in the form of casual conversation or more formal oral presentations and speeches. These latter forms of talk differ in many ways from both casual conversation and purposeful talk. Both oral presentations and speeches require the author to share their thinking in clear, concise, and engaging ways in a continuous stream, with minimal interjection from others. This means the message must be well thought out in advance. In addition, successful sharing of thinking through formal speaking necessitates a degree of confidence and control over a range of nonverbal communicative abilities, including eye contact, facial expressions, and hand gestures.

Offering children formal speaking experiences helps them build confidence with a presentation form that makes most adults weak in the knees. Their first forays into oral presentation can be contained within the safety of the classroom but should gradually extend out to larger audiences and arenas so children feel the power of ideas delivered in these ways. They might visit other classrooms to speak to other groups of students, or invite other classrooms to the auditorium for presentations that actually make use of the stage and microphones. Parents and other staff might be invited for a twist on a publishing party—the publishing of oral text.

DEBATE

When children have thought and talked their way to a strong point of view, debating someone with an opposing point of view offers another opportunity to feel the power of ideas and in-depth study. The art of debate, while different from purposeful talk, is a valued skill.

Considering debate for upper-grade children encourages them to use constructed understandings in more deliberate ways. Debate adds a layer of difficulty, in that the speaker must be both informative and persuasive while defending a point of view. This requires listening intently to a counter argument, strategizing, and drawing from a wealth and range and of preconstructed knowledge to refute that opposing point of view. Debate provides children with an opportunity to test persuasive abilities, the strength of their own convictions, and the depth of their knowledge. The chart shown in Figure 8.1 (p. 111) is a support under construction in a fourth-grade classroom preparing for their first debates. The children are working toward understanding the oral genre as they read, think, and talk among multiple sources of information on social issues in preparation.

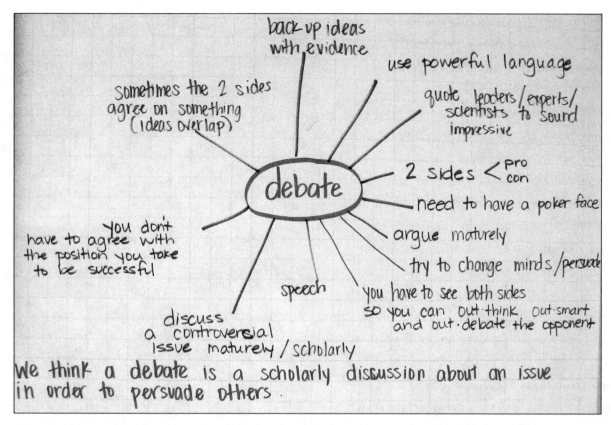

Figure 8.1: A support under construction in a fourth-grade classroom preparing for their first debates

Sharing Our Thinking in Writing

Writing is often part of the process of wrestling with big ideas. Writing forces us to grapple with our own vague, random thoughts, and articulate them in clear, concise ways. As Elie Wiesel explains, "I write to understand as much as to be understood." Wiesel clearly recognizes the dual role writing serves: it is part of the process of understanding and a means of sharing our understanding.

Writing is one of the ways we have traditionally asked children to show what they know. Written products may run the gamut from traditional forms, such as reports, feature articles, poems, or persuasive essays, to digital forms, such as blogs or postings on Web sites, or inclusion in mixed-media pieces such as PowerPoint.

POSTERS AND SIGNS

The first time Jeralyn's children shared their thinking about American heroes with those outside their classroom was when they were studying Benjamin Franklin. So enamored were they of Franklin and his discoveries and inventions that they wanted not only to share their reverence for Ben but to convince others that Ben was deserving of their admiration, too.

The children decided to design signs, which would be strategically placed around the Webster campus, prompting others to wonder at the ways Ben has touched our lives. While these signs were clearly a sharing of literal information, the children took care to craft the information in clever ways, seeing this as an opportunity to convince others of the pivotal role Ben played in shaping our world. In this way, the signs revealed the children's deeper understanding of the effect Ben and his inventions had on our world.

As we hoped, the signs, several of which are pictured in Figure 8.2, were not only noticed but soon became the talk of the campus. Webster was abuzz with questions about Ben and the authors of these sources of information. Investigations soon narrowed the search for answers to Jeralyn's students, and they became ambassadors of Franklin's accomplishments. The children talked about Ben with anyone who would listen. Teachers reported Ben Franklin books flying off library shelves, and for a short time at least, Ben was truly the big man on campus.

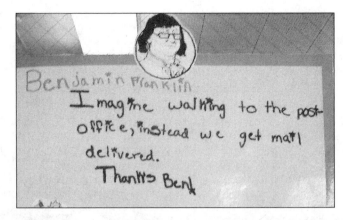

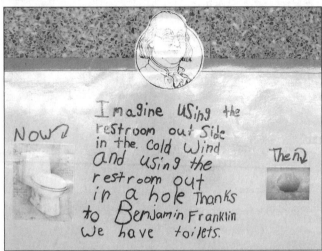

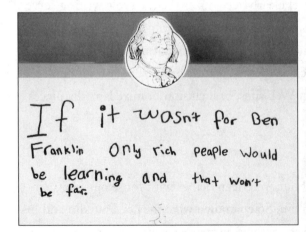

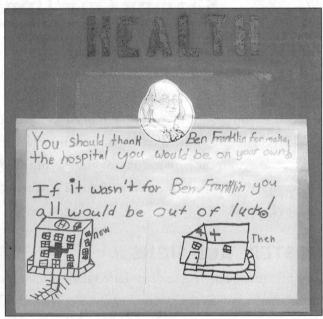

Figure 8.2: Some of the signs about Benjamin Franklin that hung around Webster school

Expanding Comprehension With Multigenre Text Sets

From this purposeful effort to put their thinking out into the world, the children learned several valuable lessons. They learned the power of an organized campaign that saturates a small market with large amounts of information in clever ways. They saw that, with effort, they had the power to inform, persuade, and entertain. And most important, they learned that their thinking, which was based on carefully constructed understandings, truly had an impact on others.

REPORTS

As briefly alluded to in Chapter 6, the writing workshop can be seamlessly integrated into the reading workshop as the children read, think, and talk among multiple sources of information. As children work toward constructing an in-depth understanding of issues and ideas, writing again can help them untangle their thinking and work toward sharing it.

Loya's report, pictured in Figure 8.3, was the result of a flow between the reading and writing workshop in a third-grade class also engaged in the "What Is an American Hero?"

Heroic Abe by Loya

Abe Lincoln was born on February 12, 1809. Back then, people had no houses like we do today. Instead, they lived in log cabins. And when they had to go to school, they only had one room. And they had slavery and that was not going to stop until . . . Abe came.

Get Up Soldier, There Is War!
This was July 1863, and here is the Civil War. The man who was president was Abraham Lincoln. Two armies fought for years. Cannons boomed. Swords flashed. There were terrible battles. The North won. Lincoln was thankful. Still, he felt sad. So many dead boys! Not one of them ready to die. "My heart is like lead," he said.

Abe Lincoln's Famous Speech
This is the speech that Abe said at Gettysburg:
Four score and seven years ago our fathers brought forth upon this continent a new nation, conceived in liberty and dedicated to the proclamation that all men are created equal. . . .

People remember his speech because he talked about ideas he believed in, and they believed him, too.

The Shocking News
Abe Lincoln was at a play and right in the middle of the play a man came up beside Abe. He was so furious for letting the slaves free that the man shot Abe right in the head. The bullet hit Abe's brain. The man's name that shot Abe was John Wilkes Booth.

President Lincoln was unconscious throughout the night. In the morning he died. His body lay in the coffin in the White House. A train took his body on a long trip back to Illinois.

Remembering Our Hero, Abe Lincoln
Abe Lincoln is a hero for everybody who believes people should have freedom. He stood for freedom for everybody even when it was hard. That's why he is a hero. They stay true to their heart.

The Lincoln Memorial was made to remind us of Abe and how he wanted freedom for all. It is on the penny so every time we spend money, we remember. We should remember and never forget so we always have freedom.

Figure 8.3: Loya's report about Abraham Lincoln

unit. Loya and her classmates wrote reports for the purpose of informing other Webster students of the role of heroes in shaping our world.

In "Heroic Abe," Loya is clearly sharing thinking about an individual she truly admires. If you had the privilege of observing Loya's process of constructing understanding in the reading workshop, you would have seen her navigating a range of sources of information with her partner. Her report, designed to inform, includes a range of facts compiled from these sources. There are strong hints at Loya's own point of view about Lincoln. What we don't have evidence of in this piece is a shift from the topic of Lincoln himself to a big idea or issue surrounding him. This does not mean this shift did not occur; it's possible that the genre of Report simply did not entice these thoughts out of Loya. To know with certainty, we simply would need to talk with her to develop a full picture of the depth of the ideas and understandings she constructed.

From a craft and qualities of writing standpoint, Loya has learned the power of quotations—both quotations of spoken language and quotations from other texts, such as speeches. She is playing with sentence fluency and elements of voice. Through this report, Loya is able to share her thinking with all of Webster, and Loya's teacher is able to take a closer look at Loya's abilities and next steps.

FEATURE ARTICLES

Feature articles allow authors a little more freedom to share their thinking in playful ways while conveying a strong point of view with efforts to persuade. The genre encourages the exploration of big ideas and issues surrounding a topic, offering authors the opportunity to use the full scope of their expanded comprehension to affect their readers.

Feature articles designed with an attractive page layout and incorporating a range of text features are also visually appealing. When displayed on a bulletin board in a public access area of the campus, they become traffic stoppers for students and parents alike. As the children watch others pausing to read their articles, they again realize their potential to affect others.

ESSAYS

Many upper-grade classrooms look to essays as a means of having children share their thinking from work inside units that draw from multiple sources of information. Essay is an ideal genre for sharing knowledge constructed through reading, thinking, and talking among sources of information, as both the essay and the process of reading, thinking, and talking among multiple sources to expand comprehension are journeys of thought. The crafting of an essay offers children an opportunity to retrace the development of their own point of view in a way that invites the reader to join in. This results in strongly persuasive pieces, complete with an awareness of opposing points of view and compelling arguments against them.

POEMS

Many children take great joy in writing poetry, particularly free verse. When children include rich poetry alive with big ideas about the world and poems about real people and events in their text sets, they begin to view poetry as an alternate means of sharing their own thinking with the world. When offered the opportunity, many will choose poetry to share their thinking with others.

Nicole's poem, "I Feel Your Wind," shown in Figure 8.4, reveals her respect for Amelia Earhart, an understanding of Earhart's contributions to society, and an aspiration to live a heroic life herself. She was able to pack a lot of power into very few words—a sign of strength as a writer.

Sharing Our Thinking Through Twenty-first Century Media Forms

Access to technology varies greatly in schools across the United States. Despite the difference in current situations, the trend nationally is towards greater access for all. Digital cameras, camcorders, and laptops are slowly becoming the norm rather than the exception, with interactive whiteboards looming on the horizon.

Some schools are set up with technology labs where children learn to use the devices and their supporting software; in other situations, teachers are offering how-to instruction with the technology as children work to incorporate technology as a tool for constructing meaning and sharing their thinking.

DIGITAL STILL SHOTS

One of my favorite television commercials these days is of a four-and-a-half-year-old explaining to her audience how she connects her digital camera to the computer and downloads still shots. Aimed at the company's opponent in the computing platform wars, this commercial was crafted to convey how easy working with digital still shots has become. Not all kindergartners arrive with this skill set, but when digital cameras are available for use, we can certainly begin incorporating them into children's efforts to share their thinking with others.

I Feel Your Wind
By Nicole

You changed my life,
Amelia
The first woman
Of the sky.

I believe in you,
Amelia
The bravest woman
We needed.

I am determined,
Amelia
And brave
I feel you.

Thank you
Amelia Earhart.

Figure 8.4: Nicole's poem about Amelia Earhart

With access to digital cameras, the poster campaign in Jeralyn's class could easily have morphed into a photographic essay highlighting Benjamin Franklin's inventions and social contributions, and emphasizing their impact on our world today. By adding photographs imported from the Web, a before-and-after format becomes a possibility. Our fifth grade's co-constructed understanding of perseverance could as well have been expressed through a photo essay.

Creating texts with digital still shots can be carried out via a shared approach, with the teacher supporting the technology and the children working together to craft the message. Or, it could just as easily be approached through group or individual projects. What's important is that children recognize still shots as a powerful support to a message rather than simply decoration.

POWERPOINT

PowerPoint provides a digital means of sharing text and images, and the possibility of musical accompaniment to boot. Using PowerPoint (or other presentation software), children are able to work with multiple media forms to create a text that is visually appealing. They also learn the power of graphics in sending their message out into the world.

Again, crafting messages in PowerPoint can begin in a shared approach with our younger learners and, depending on access to computers, become group and individual projects in upper grades. Learning to format slides in ways that support a message as opposed to overpowering it, developing an awareness of quantity and size of texts on slides, considering the slide design—all of these aspects are part of learning to use PowerPoint to its fullest potential.

VIDEO

Camcorders create a whole new realm of possibility for sharing thinking. Video has the potential to blend the impact of speaking directly and passionately about one's beliefs with the possibility of wider distribution of a message, touching a more diverse audience. In 2008, as a class project, high school students at Village Academy High School in Pomona, California, made a video sharing their realities and fears as they relate to the severe economic downturn. They posted their video, titled *Is Anybody Listening?* on YouTube. Among the somebodies who were listening was one particular somebody— President Barack Obama. President Obama referred to this film in a speech on education delivered on March 19, 2009, actually quoting one of the students. A week after his speech, while touring California, Obama stopped to meet the students face to face.

Whether this opportunity to share their thinking with the President will change these students' realities remains to be seen. However, the opportunity does illustrate the power of using new technologies to share your thinking with the world. It's important to note that video does not need to be posted online to have an impact. Imagine a family film night, with families filling the auditorium for video screenings—a localized version of the Sundance Film Festival.

When using technology as a means of supporting children in sending their thinking out into the world, our aim is always to use it in a way that draws from its full potential. Access to technology should add depth to the ideas presented, either through access to a greater range of sources of information, or by adding visuals that are sources of information themselves, thereby strengthening the message. The end result should be a far more powerful message than could have been achieved using paper and pencil.

When children experience a wide range of ways to send carefully constructed messages based on thoughtful learning out into the world, they develop a repertoire of potential strategies for igniting change. In this way, a curriculum of thought begets a life of action. It is through such action—from modeling the quest to live heroically to sharing ideas that open eyes and minds—that we rise to meet the challenges of an ever changing world.

Epilogue

An informed citizenry is at the heart of a dynamic democracy.
~Thomas Jefferson

In an op-ed piece titled "The Daily Me" (*New York Times*, March 19, 2009), Nicholas Kristof writes, ". . . there's pretty good evidence that we generally don't truly want good information—but rather information that confirms our prejudices. We may believe intellectually in the clash of opinions, but in practice we like to embed ourselves in the reassuring womb of an echo chamber." In this piece, Kristof discusses the dangers of a public able to serve as their own gatekeeper for information as they turn in greater numbers to online sources for news. Most people, Kristof argues, engage in "selective truth seeking." Essentially, he says, we prefer news that supports our own point of view, whether thoughtfully conceived or not.

The danger in this, of course, is that, by narrowing our intake of information to a single point of view, we naturally become very narrow in our thinking. By stifling other voices, we turn our backs on opportunities to think and talk purposefully with others who have the diverse perspectives necessary to expand our own thinking. The end result of this narrow-mindedness is an inability to innovate and problem solve.

Our goal in teaching children to read, think, and talk among multiple sources of information is to create individuals with the abilities and the inclination to do exactly the opposite—expand their thinking by drawing from a range of sources and perspectives, thus nurturing their innovative and problem-solving potential. As Kristof suggests, our solution to a society ruled by narrow-mindedness is to "struggle on our own to work out intellectually with sparring partners whose views we deplore." While we hope our children develop a healthier respect for alternative points of view than Kristof suggests, we aim towards developing the habits of mind to purposefully seek out a range of sources of information and points of view.

When children engage in the process of reading, thinking, and talking among multiple sources of information in the pursuit of big ideas, they are learning strategies for taking on the big ideas and issues they will encounter both in and out of school, now and forever. They learn to respect other points of view, draw from them as a means of opening up their own thinking, expanding their understanding and gradually forming their own well-thought-through point of view. Children learn to become creators of knowledge rather than sponges for other's ideas.

Through these efforts, we are creating individuals who are able to contribute thoughtfully to society. An informed citizenry, as Jefferson suggests, is essential and requires a strong understanding of the process necessary to understand complex ideas and issues, the habits of mind required to strive continuously for understanding, and the propensity to act upon that understanding with an eye toward the greater good. The end result is truly a dynamic democracy.

Appendix A: Reading Unit of Inquiry Overview

Essential questions						
Desired results						
What to Teach	Why	Instructional Approach	Sources of Information	What might talk indicative of strong comprehension sound like?	What might talk indicative of strong reading, thinking, and talking among sources sound like?	

Appendix B: Week-long Instruction

Unit: _____ Week: _____

Whole-class instruction				
Partner and independent work				

Afterword

What is the point of education if not to prepare children for life? Maria Nichols describes what that means and how to accomplish it while ostensibly merely "expanding comprehension." Maria plans literacy instruction backwards from the demands of an advanced and rapidly changing democratic society that requires increasingly creative and collaborative problem-solving. She shows us why it is important to engage children in dialogic conversations, and why they should engage multiple sources. One is an extension of the other. To understand a text deeply, we need multiple perspectives. To understand a subject, idea, or concept more deeply, we need multiple texts because each text offers another author's perspective on the subject.

Maria shows in detail how to use and construct text sets, and how, particularly through the children's conversations, they improve comprehension. These conversations are demanding, yet we hear quite young children not only engaging in them, but becoming independent in initiating and managing them. She shows us how to set up multiple text sets, but she also shows us how to teach children to set them up—to gather and analyze multiple relevant texts—to do research.

Maria shows us how to engage in evidence-based instruction closely linked to both short-and long-term goals. She shows us where to find the evidence and how to use it in our planning. On the one hand, this is demanding teaching. It requires rigorous planning. On the other, it provides excitement—teaching that doesn't feel like work. She knows that teaching this way takes more time but she shows us how to get that time by accomplishing more at once, for example, by combining subject area teaching—making literacy learning not simply an end in itself, but something one does in order to learn about and accomplish something.

It helps to choose interesting texts, but the key to building dialogic conversations around texts and text sets is in the ways we as teachers talk with children. The teachers help children understand what they are doing (not merely reading), who they are, and what to value. For example, take Jeralyn's comment to her students after their conversation about George Washington. As Maria points out, Jeralyn "wanted to be sure all children were aware of what they had just accomplished by thinking and talking together, and how."

> "So, it sounds as if we're thinking that George Washington was quite brave. This conversation started because Toya questioned George's behavior. Manuel pushed back by reminding us of the time George lived in—the way of the world back then. So, you questioned, you were flexible with your thinking, and you used an important strategy for understanding biographies—considering the person in the time that he or she lived in. Let's keep reading and see if your thinking grows or changes."

Turning children's attention to the process and the consequence of that process, she foregrounds the children's thinking. She offers them an identity as thinkers, both as individuals, and as a thinking community—a community that includes herself ("we're"). She points to the process that led to the interesting conversation highlighting the value of questioning and "pushing back"—providing a counter argument, and disagreement, at the same time showing the value of difference. She poses their conclusion as tentative ("it sounds as if"), which leaves room for the children to work further on the idea, to decide for themselves whether they support the claim. This encourages them to develop a sense of agency in their knowledge production. She also makes clear what they are doing—they are working towards "growing and changing their thinking."

The foundation this instruction provides for children includes building a tolerance for ambiguity and uncertainty, a foundation that will allow them not only to keep a conversation open and treat each other with respect, but to keep their minds open. This, and the necessary perspective taking, is more important than we think. It affects children's moral development, such as their likelihood of being prejudiced and their ability to resolve social problems productively.

Maria and the teachers she works with offer us a vision of what is possible in schools when we take children and their future seriously. She shows us why we must take this path if our children are to survive the future, and she offers the necessary maps of different scales to help us get there. We are not just teaching a bunch of separate minds, but a society of minds.

—Peter Johnston
Albany, New York

References

Afflerbach, P., & VanSledright, B. (1998, December). The challenge of understanding the past: How do fifth grade readers construct meaning from diverse history texts? Paper presented at the annual meeting of the National Reading Conference, Austin, TX.

Akhavan, N. (2004). *How to align literacy instruction, assessment, and standards and achieve results you never dreamed possible.* Portsmouth, NH: Heinemann.

Allington, R. L. (2001). *What really matters for struggling readers.* New York: Addison-Wesley Educational Publishers.

Allington, R. (2002). You can't learn much from books you can't read. *Educational Leadership, 60*(3), 16–19.

Anderson, C. (2000). *How's it going?: A practical guide to conferring with student writers.* Portsmouth, N.H.: Heinemann.

Berra, Y., & Kaplan, D. (2001). *When you come to a fork in the road, take it.* New York: Hyperion.

Blachowitz, C., & Ogle, D. (2001). *Reading comprehension: Strategies for independent learning.* New York: Guilford.

Bohm, D. (1996). *On dialogue.* New York: Routledge.

Brown, R. (1991). *Schools of thought: How the politics of literacy shape thinking in the classroom.* San Francisco: Jossey-Bass.

Browne, M. N., & Keeley, S. M. (2004). *Asking the right questions: A guide to critical thinking.* Upper Saddle River, NJ: Pearson Education.

Cazden, C. (2001). *Classroom discourse: The language of teaching and learning.* Portsmouth, NH: Heinemann.

Collier, P. (2007). *The bottom line: Why the poorest countries are failing and what can be done about it.* New York: Oxford University Press.

Costa, A. L., & Liebmann, R. L. (1997). *The process-centered school: Sustaining a renaissance community.* Thousand Oaks, CA: Corwin Press.

Covey, S. (1990). *The 7 habits of highly effective people.* New York: Free Press.

Dweck, C. (2006). *Mindset: The new psychology of success.* New York: Random House.

Freebody, P., & Luke, A. (1990). Literacies' programmes: Debates and demands in cultural contexts. *Prospect: A Journal of Australian TESOL* 11:7–16.

Freire, P. (1970). *Pedagogy of the oppressed.* New York: The Seabury Press.

Gardner, H. (2006). *Five minds for the future.* Boston: Harvard Business School Press.

Graham, A. (2005, January 9). Worst-case scenarios. *The Washington Post*, p. BW05.

Harste, J. (June 18, 2006). Understanding reading: Multiple perspectives, multiple insights. Retrieved October 7, 2008 from http://php.indiana.edu/~harste/wrkprg/UnderstandingReading.pdf.

Jetton, T. L. (1994). Information vs. story driven: What children remember when they read informational stories. *Reading Psychology, 15*, 109–130.

Johnston, P. (2004). *Choice words: How our language affects children's learning.* Portland, ME: Stenhouse.

Keene, E. (2008). *To understand.* Portsmouth, NH: Heinemann.

Kelley, T., & Littman, J. (2001). *The art of innovation.* New York: Doubleday.

Kristof, N. (2009, March 19). The daily me. *The New York Times,* p. A31.

Laminack, L., & Wadsworth, R. M. (2006). *Reading aloud across the curriculum.* Portsmouth, NH: Heinemann.

Lattimer, H. (2003). *Thinking through genre: Units of study in reading and writing workshops 4–12.* Portland, ME: Stenhouse.

Luke, A. (1994). *The social construction of literacy in the classroom.* Melbourne, AU: Macmillan.

Moje, E. B. (1996). I teach students, not subjects: Teacher-student relationships as contexts for secondary literacy. *Reading Research Quarterly, 31,* 172–195.

Mooney, M. (2001). *Text forms and features: A resource for intentional teaching.* Katonah, NY: Richard C. Owens.

Morgan, N., & Saxton, J. (2006). *Asking better questions.* Ontario, Canada: Pembroke.

National Center on Education and the Economy. (2006). *Tough choices or tough times: The report of the New Commission on the Skills of the American Workforce.* San Francisco: Jossey-Bass.

Nichols, M. (2006). *Comprehension through conversation: The power of purposeful talk in the reading workshop.* Portsmouth, N.H.: Heinemann.

Nichols, M. (2008). *Talking about text: Guiding students to increase comprehension through purposeful talk.* Huntington Beach, CA: Shell Publishing.

Noddings, N. (2008). All our students thinking. *Educational Leadership, 65*(5), 9–13.

Ogle, D., & Blachowitz, C. (2002). Beyond literature circles: Helping students comprehend informational texts. In C. C. Block & M. Pressley (Eds.), *Comprehension instruction: Research-based best practices.* New York: Guilford.

Opitz, M. F., Ford, M. P., & Zbaracki, M. D. (2006). *Books and beyond: New ways to reach readers.* Portsmouth, NH: Heinemann.

Pearson, P. D. (2001, December). *What we have learned in 30 years.* Paper presented at the 51st annual meeting of the National Reading Conference, San Antonio, TX.

Perkins, D. (1995). *Smart schools: Better thinking and learning for every child.* New York: The Free Press.

Perkins, D. (2008). Creating thought-full environments. In A. L. Costa & B. Kallick (Eds.), *Learning and leading with habits of mind: 16 essential characteristics for success.* Danvers, MA: Association for Supervision and Curriculum Development.

Peterson, R. (1992). *Life in a crowded place: Making a learning community.* Portsmouth, NH: Heinemann.

Posner, R. (2006). *Uncertain shield: The U.S. intelligence system in the throes of reform.* Lanham, MD: Roman & Littlefield Publishers.

Resnick, L. (1999). *Making America smarter. Education Week Century Series 18*(40); 38–40. Retrieved November 14, 2008 from http://ifl.lrdc.pitt.edu/ifl/media/pdf/MakingAmericaSmarter.pdf

Richgels, D. J. (December 1997). *Informational texts in kindergarten: reading and writing to learn.* Paper presented at the meeting of the National Reading Conference, Scottsdale, Arizona.

Robb, L. (2002). Multiple texts: Multiple opportunities for teaching and learning. *Voices from the Middle, 9*(4), 28–32.

Sachs, J. D. (2005). *The end of poverty: Economic possibilities for our time.* New York: Penguin.

Sen, A. (1999). *Development as freedom.* New York: Random House.

Shirky, C. (2008). *Here comes everybody: The power of organizing without organizations.* New York: Penguin.

Shanahan, C. (2003). *Using multiple texts to teach content*. Retrieved January 17, 2009, from http://www.learningpt.org/pdfs/literacy/shanahan.

Simpson, M. L., & Nist, S. L. (2002). Encouraging active reading at the college level. In C. C. Block and M. Pressley (Eds.), *Comprehension instruction: Research-based best practices* (pp. 365–379). New York: Guilford.

Spandel, V. (2001). *Creating writers through 6-trait writing assessment and instruction*. New York: Addison Wesley Longman.

Stead, T. (2006). *Reality checks: Teaching reading comprehension with nonfiction K–5*. Portland, ME: Stenhouse.

Wiggins, G., & McTighe, J. (1998). *Understanding by design*. Alexandria, VA: Association for Supervision and Curriculum Development.

Wineburg, S. S. (1991). On the reading of historical texts: Notes on the breach between school and academy. *America Educational Research Journal, 28*(3), 495–519.

Wineburg, S. S. (2001). *Historical thinking and other unnatural acts: Charting the future of teaching the past*. Philadelphia: Temple University Press.

Children's Literature Cited

Abraham, P. (2002). *Benjamin Franklin*. Mexico: Rosen Books.

Anderson, L. (September 30, 2008). Amazing aquatics: Hundreds of new animal species discovered off the coast of Australia. *Scholastic News*. Retrieved October 17, 2008, from http://www2.scholastic.com/browse/article.jsp?id=3750430.

Berger, M. (1999). *Chomp! A book about sharks*. New York: Scholastic.

Bishop, G. (2002, June 1). Swimming with sharks. In *Ranger Rick*, National Wildlife Federation.

Brisson, P. (1999). *The summer my father was ten*. Honesdale, PA: Boyds Mills Press.

Brown, J. A. (2005). *Henry Ford*. Milwaukee, WI: Weekly Reader Early Learning Library.

Bunting, E. (1989). *The Wednesday surprise*. New York: Clarion.

Bunting, E. (1992). *The wall*. New York: Clarion.

Bunting, E. (1998). *So far from the sea*. Boston: Houghton Mifflin Harcourt.

Bunting, E. (2000). *Memory string*. New York: Clarion.

Bunting, E. (2001). *Gleam and glow*. San Diego, CA: Harcourt.

Burleigh, R. (2003). *Amelia Earhart: Fire in the skies*. China: Harcourt.

Chandra, D., & Comora, M. (2003). *George Washington's teeth*. New York: Farrar Straus Giroux.

Cheney, L. (2004). *When Washington crossed the Delaware: A wintertime story for young patriots*. New York: Simon & Schuster.

Chin-Lee, C. (2005). *Amelia to Zora: Twenty-six women who changed the world*. Watertown, MA: Charlesbridge.

Cooper, F. (2004). *Jump! From the life of Michael Jordan*. New York: Philomel.

Cooper, M. L. (2002). *Remembering Manzanar: Life in a Japanese relocation camp*. New York: Clarion.

Coy, J. (1999). *Strong to the hoop*. New York: Lee and Low.

Fleischman, P. (2002). *Seedfolks*. New York: Harper Trophy.

Fletcher, R. (1999). "Teamwork" from *Relatively speaking*. New York: Orchard.

Giovanni, N. (2005). *Rosa*. New York: Henry Holt.

Graves, D. (1996). "The Accident" from *Baseball, snakes, and summer squash*. Honesdale, PA: Boyds Mills.

Hardin, W. (1997). *Henry Ford Museum: An ABC of American innovation*. New York: Henry N. Abrams.

Harness, C. (2000). *George Washington*. Washington, DC: National Geographic Society.

Henkes, K. (1995). *Julius, the baby of the world*. Hong Kong: HarperCollins.

Holzer, H. (2000). *Abraham Lincoln the writer: A treasury of his greatest speeches and letters*. Honesdale, PA: Boyds Mills Press.

Howard, E. F. (2001). *Aunt Flossie's hats (and crab cakes later)*. New York: Clarion.

Hunter, S. H. (1996). *The unbreakable code*. Flagstaff, AZ: Rising Moon.

Johnston, T., & Mazellan, R. (2007). *The harmonica*. Watertown, MA: Charlesbridge.

Keats, E. J. (1967). *Peter's chair*. New York: Penguin.

Kulling, M. (2004). *Eat my dust!: Henry Ford's first race*. New York: Random House.

Mara, W. (2002). *Amelia Earhart*. New York: Scholastic.

Mara, W. (2003). *Henry Ford*. New York: Scholastic.

McCutcheon, J. (2006). *Christmas in the trenches*. Atlanta, GA: Peachtree.

Mochizuki, K. (1993). *Baseball Saved Us*. New York: Lee and Low.

New York Times Magazine. (July 3, 1937). "Miss Earhart forced down at sea, Howland Isle fears; Coast Guard begins search." Retrieved April 3, 2009, from http://www.nytimes.com/specials/magazine4/articles/earhart1.html

Polacco, P. (1992). *Chicken Sunday*. New York: Putnam.

Polacco, P. (1998). *My rotten redheaded older brother*. New York: Aladdin.

Polacco, P. (2007). *The lemonade club*. New York: Philomel.

Rosenthal, M., & Freeman, D. (1999). *Amelia Earhart*. Mankato, MN: Capstone Press.

Ryan, P. M. (1999). *Amelia and Eleanor go for a ride*. New York: Scholastic.

Schaefer, L. M. (1999). *George Washington*. Mankato, MN: Capstone Press.

Schanzer, R. (2002). *How Ben Franklin stole the lightning*. China: HarperCollins.

Smith, L. (2006). *John, Paul, George & Ben*. New York: Hyperion.

Spalding, A., & Wilson, J. (1999). *Me and Mr. Mah*. Toronto, Ontario: Orca Books.

Time for Kids editors, with Satterfield, K. H. (2005). *Benjamin Franklin: A man of many talents*. China: HarperCollins.

Uchida, Y. (1996). *The bracelet*. New York: Paperstar.

Venezia, M. (2004). *George Washington: First president*. New York: Scholastic.

Wickham, M. (1997). *Mysterious journey: Amelia Earhart's last flight*. Norwalk, CT: Trudy Corporation.

Woodson, J. (2001). *The other side*. New York: Putnam.

Woodson, J. (2002). *Our Gracie aunt*. New York: Hyperion.

Yolen, J. (1987). *Owl moon*. New York: Philomel.